Paradox

Paradox

by Gideon Rappaport

One Mind Good Press
San Diego, California

One Mind Good Press
San Diego, CA 92117

ISBN: 979-8-218-50059-7

"Look at all the works of the Most High; they come in pairs, one the opposite of the other."

—Ecclesiasticus 33:15

"If you can't live with paradox, you're going to have a hard life."

—Mary Holmes

"We can't comprehend what comprehends us."

—Wendell Berry

Contents

Preface: What Is Paradox? ix

1. Consciousness and Self-Consciousness 1

2. Transcendence and Immanence 3

3. Justice and Mercy 6

4. Finite and Infinite 8

5. *Halacha* and *Kabbala* 10

6. Free Will and Predetermination 15

7. Time and Eternity 18

8. Body and Soul 19

9. Knowledge and Faith... 25

10. Community and Individual.. 27

11. Pattern-Discerning and Pattern-Making 29

12. Plato and Aristotle 31

13. General and Particular... 33

14. Form and Content 35

15. Empathy and Psychic Distance... 42

16. Beauty: Promise and Temptation... 45

17. Male and Female 47

18. Sex and Love 49

19. Self and Loss of Self... 50

20. Journey and Destination.. 53

21. Integrity and Change 55

22. Right and Responsibility 57

23. Caring and Not Caring... 60

24. Is Denmark a Prison? 62

25. Athens and Jerusalem 65

26. Yang and Yin 68

27. Being and Non-Being..77

Preface: What Is Paradox?

The etymology of the word *paradox* is instructive. *Para* in Greek means beside, alongside of, and thereby can also mean amiss or wrong. *Dox* comes from the Greek *dokein*, meaning to think, suppose, imagine, conjecture, expect, and also to seem. The noun made from the verb, *doxa*, can therefore mean notion, opinion, expectation, sentiment, judgment; also conjecture; and from these senses it also comes to mean estimation, reputation, popular or received opinion. Hence the Greek word *paradoxos* means alongside or contrary to received opinion, against expectation, incredible. A *paradoxologia* was a tale of wonder, a marvel, and a *paradoxopoeia* was a wonder-working, a miracle.

In English, the oldest sense of the word *paradox* is the figure of speech falling under the heading of logical contraries and contradictories, namely an opinion, statement, or tenet contrary to that of most men and to received opinion, often with the additional sense of being unbelievable or wondrous. To that sense of the rhetorical figure was added the sense of self-contradiction, as in Troilus's statement "This is, and is not, Cressid!" (*Troilus and Cressida*, V.ii.146) or Iago's "I am not what I am" (*Othello*, I.i.65) or Cordelia's "No cause, no cause" (*King Lear*, IV.vii.74) when she has very good cause.

In modern English, *paradox* can mean a statement that is seemingly contradictory or opposed to common sense and yet is perhaps true, or a self-contradictory statement that seems true but also seems to contradict the law of non-contradiction fundamental to Aristotelian logic, which states that the same thing cannot be both A and not-A in the same respect at the same time. Hidden in both senses lurks the sense of marvel, wonder, or miracle.

Notice that *paradox* in the sense of logical self-contradiction does not simply mean opposites, though opposites may seem in thought to imply paradox or bring us in experience to confront it. In the *Phaedo*, Plato has Socrates observe that pleasure and pain cannot both be felt at the same time, yet to have the one is almost always to have the other also, like two bodies with one head.

> I am sure that if Aesop had thought of it he would have made up a fable about them, something like this: God wanted to stop their continual quarreling, and when he found that it was impossible, he

fastened their heads together; so wherever one of them appears, the other is sure to follow after.[1]

Socrates' pleasure and pain do not themselves form a paradox in the sense of a self-contradictory statement, though they are opposites. But that they are experienced close together, one appearing close upon the other, seems paradoxical, as it did to Socrates. Night and day are opposites, too, but they do not form a paradox of self-contradiction because the alternation of light and dark is not self-contradictory, given the facts of time and motion: If we assume that the earth rotates in time in its orbit around the sun, we can accept the realities of night and day without difficulty. Youth and age are at opposite ends of the timeline of human life, but they are not mutually exclusive in any one life of threescore and ten years. Likewise, hunger and satiety, alternating with one another, though they are opposites, form no self-contradiction. Pleasure and pain, light and dark, youth and age, hunger and satiety can all be true without perplexing the mind perforce.

With paradox, however, the two heads fastened together in Socrates' version of an Aesop fable would appear not one following after another but absolutely together. In contrast to mere opposites, a paradox in this sense cannot *not* perplex the mind. Paradox confronts us with the question whether something that is the opposite of what is true can also be true at the same time and in the same respect. How can the same phenomenon be both wave and particle? How can God be both transcendent and immanent?

What happens to us when we perceive the equal and simultaneous truth of diametrically opposed contradictory realities? When we are forced by experience and thought to conclude that the impossible must also be possible? The experience of paradox in this sense is not about coming to believe nonsense. It is about coming to recognize that two absolutely contradictory facts, experiences, or ideas may have absolutely equal claims to validity. What happens to us when we arrive at that recognition?

Sometimes we turn against one of the two opposed truths and deny it, assuming that we've missed something in coming to what seemed like a necessary conclusion. Sometimes we throw up our hands, perhaps after railing against the injustice or absurdity of our fate, and leave the

---

1   60c, translated by Hugh Tredennick.

problem to better minds than ours. And sometimes, if we exercise careful discernment, we are forced to ask about such paradoxes of human life, "is one impossible without the other such that they are, in relationship, part of one thing, and that of a third kind?" and why and "how are we ever surprised by the recognition of sameness in difference that points over and over to the continuity of opposites and the ultimate unity of these universal paradoxes?"[2] Paradox forces us to engage our capacity for discernment, and then drives our discernment to its limit at the borders of mystery, where we are compelled to intuit a dimension of reality in which the opposites can both be true without self-contradiction or absurdity, a dimension in which the equal truth of the contraries actually makes sense. Cressida is Cressida, but she isn't who Troilus thought she was. Iago is not what he appears to be to the other characters; to the audience he is a demonic opposite of God, who says, "I am that I am" (Exodus 3:14). Yes, the story of her life gives Cordelia good cause; but in her soul she perceives "No cause, no cause."

Professor Mary Holmes called paradox "the natural condition of the world. It is both the working principle and the mystery of life… We are always surrounded by paradox because all of creation is the union of opposites. All energy comes from the union of opposites."[3] Holmes is here tying our experience of paradox to our consciousness of opposites. And her insight reminds us that though our human categories of thought are insufficient to contain all of reality, yet our experience of paradoxical contraries invites us to ask: What is the unity that binds these opposites into relation to one another, that reveals two mutual exclusives as paradoxically parts of one underlying reality?

The following observations consider without finality some of the fundamental contraries that we human persons experience as paradoxes in contemplating ourselves and the world. We think about them because we want, perhaps need, to do so. Also perhaps because we are meant to be joined to one another in shared contemplation of that mysterious unity of which (paradoxically) we are all members.

*　*　*

I am deeply grateful to Bruce Cantz and Christopher Maron for

---

2 Christopher Maron, privately.

3 Addi Somekh and Charlie Eckert, *Mary Holmes: Paintings and Ideas* (Los Altos, CA: Very Press, 2002), page 117.

fruitful conversations on these topics. My thanks go also to copy editor Tom Feltham, book designer Chuck Eng, and proofreader Mark Swift. Blind spots and blunders are mine.

1. Consciousness and Self-Consciousness

A human self, almost by definition, not only can observe itself. It can also observe itself observing itself. But not for very long. Attempting to keep at that feat leads to mental paralysis or to changing the subject—that is, changing the object of thought. As with the young thinker's attempt to imagine an end to infinite space and then to imagine what is beyond that, thinking about our own thinking leads us into a recursive loop that ends in stasis and consequent boredom, which, in a mock advertisement, the poet Philip Thompson called "the largest of blessings in disguise."[1] We turn to mental pursuits likely to yield more meaningful fruit.

And yet we are aware of ourselves as both a consciousness and an object of consciousness. We ask questions like "Why did I do that?" Is the "I" asking the question the same as the "I" who did the deed? If so, why is the question necessary? Does the doer know the answer that the asker does not? If so, what is the difference between the asker and the doer? Are we two selves in one? Or more than two? For we might ask, "Why am I asking myself that question?" Now we seem to have a doer, an asker, and an asker of the asker. Do we have three selves in one? Or an infinite regress of selves? "Why am I asking myself why I am asking myself that question?" etc. We know that such a line of questions can go on, but it must end either in laughter and surrender to the mystery or in madness.

At moments we may respond to the awareness of ourselves with wonder and awe and joy. At those moments, humbled, we may be moved to give thanks. And then we turn our attention to some labor or goal or effort to merit the gift of that wonder that is our own consciousness, to turn it to account in some invisible imagined ledger. But if we attempt to keep our consciousness focused on itself, we cannot help falling into misery at the awareness of our imperfections, our limitations, our failures, our physical pains, our impending death. And that ongoing misery can easily turn to frustration, resentment, and despair. From a joy-inspiring

---

1   Philip Thompson, "Universal Commercials," in *Dusk and Dawn: Poems and Prose of Philip Thompson*, edited by Gideon Rappaport (San Diego: One Mind Good Press, 2005), page 244.

gift our self-consciousness can turn into a slough of despond.

The natural movement of our consciousness, which cannot fail to include awareness of ourselves, is also, unless we fall into despair, a movement away from self toward something else. Focus of our consciousness upon self becomes misery; focus of our consciousness upon something else is the pursuit of meaning.

So I am a paradox to myself, and you are a paradox to yourself. And our survival depends on being able to live with that paradox, for apparently we cannot either resolve it or live without it. The attempt of the subjective self to rid itself permanently of the objective self may lead to nirvana, as in Buddhist teaching, but it may equally lead to suicide. The attempt of the objective self to rid itself permanently of the subjective self leads to psychotropic drug-taking, to danger sports like climbing Mt. Everest, or again to outright suicide. These attempts are not the same thing as the temporary escape from self and return that we crave and seek, and that we find in worship, art, play, love, and sleep, through which (at their best) we become more ourselves rather than less (see "Self and Loss of Self," page 50). Rather, the attempts at radical ridding strive to break apart the very structure, invisible and incomprehensible though it is, of the human self. Success at them is the same as death. Failure at them returns us to our paradoxical selves, perhaps humbled, but at least forced to be interested in other, more rewarding objects of thought.

This severe limitation on our capacity to make our own consciousness the fruitful object of thought might raise the question whether we, in all our complexity and paradoxical mystery, are meant to be mysteries to ourselves. Is our subject/object self itself the object of the contemplation of a higher consciousness than we can comprehend? For only a higher consciousness could possibly comprehend us. Are we structured such that, hungering for meaning and stymied in our attempts to find it in a comprehension of ourselves, we are driven to seek meaning elsewhere, to find it in relation—to another, to the world, to whatever commands our attention? Are we created to seek meaning in relating, without comprehension, to that which comprehends us?

2. Transcendence and Immanence

> Who among all the work of your hands, those above and those below,
> can say to you what are You doing? Our Father in heaven,
> do with us kindness...[1]

Speaking about God, philosophers in the world's wisdom traditions use the words and phrases "infinite," "outside of time," "outside of space," "inconceivable," "ineffable," "absolute," "transcendent." In Plato, the closest one gets to defining God is "the Form of the Good." In the descendants of Aristotle among philosophers and theologians, God is called the *Ens Perfectissimum*. For Maimonides, "no definition can be given of God" and "attributes...cannot be employed in reference to God." In Kabbala, God is called the *Ein Sof* (No End), or *Ayin* (Nothing)— meaning not that there is no God, but that to human perception God must be "not there." God is called the "First Cause,"[2] "an infinite sphere whose center is everywhere and whose circumference is nowhere,"[3] "that being than which none greater can be conceived."[4] All of these attempts to name the unnamable serve to indicate the divine reality that is the source and ground (also insufficient metaphors) of all that we call reality: time and space; matter, energy, and spirit; the universe of being and beings; consciousness; order itself. As Wendell Berry says, "we can't comprehend what comprehends us."[5] The human mind being limited, it cannot contain the unlimited. So the God of the philosophers in the intellectually elaborated spiritual traditions remains an abstract idea or

---

1   From the morning prayers in the Hebrew prayer book, where the same verb appears paradoxically in both sentences: *ma t'aseh*—present/future interrogative ("what will you do?") or indicative indirect discourse ("what you will do")—and *asay chesed*—imperative ("do kindness"). In short, no one *can* say but we *do* say.

2   Aristotle, Thomas Aquinas, and many others (cf., the cosmological argument).

3   First appearing in the twelfth-century *Book of the 24 Philosophers*, the phrase has been attributed to Aristotle, Hermes Trismegistus, Marius Victorinus, and Alain de Lille, and has been quoted by many including Pascal, Voltaire, and Johann Gottfried Herder, who calls it "the old metaphor."

4   Anselm (cf. the ontological argument).

5   Wendell Berry, *Life Is a Miracle* (Washington, D.C.: Counterpoint, 2000), page 34.

principle or concept whose referent is inconceivable by the human mind. God is transcendent.

However:

Here we are, either temporarily or permanently existent beings who must and will worship. We will worship God, or his incarnations if any (as the multiple avatars of Brahman in Hinduism, or Buddha in Mahayana Buddhism, or Jesus in Christianity). And if not God, we will worship the stars or nature or reason or knowledge or emotion or pleasure or sex or comfort or art or power or money or the past or the future or the self or some other idol, whatever we deeply believe to be at the top of our hierarchy of values, each as if it were God. That, whatever we may think, we *will* worship implies that we exist in relation to that divine Other which we worship. And if, not being guilty of idolatry, we exist in relation to God, then God must, in some unimaginable sense of which we can speak only metaphorically, be in some relation to us. A pure, inconceivable abstraction does not create a world, or address consciousness, or to it convey, whether structurally (as in Taoism) or by revelation (as in the Western religions), a moral law intended to impose on human beings alone the responsibility for choice-making between good and evil. The God to whom worshippers pray—for benefits; for mercy; for love, justice, and peace; for forgiveness of sin; for revelation of truth; for inspiration; for redemption from time, space, anguish, and death—cannot be addressed as an ineffable abstraction without qualities, cannot be worshipped as *Ayin*. For the human impulse to pray can be experienced in relation not to an inconceivable abstraction but only to a consciousness, infinitely greater than our own, yet like our own—that of man created in the image of God. We pray to God with a consciousness conscious of nothing if not of a being-in-relation with an infinite being who is Someone, or rather *the* One. So either all worship is universal illusion, or God is not only the *Ayin* but also the Creator who promises us ultimate meaning in lives charged with principles. And since human beings will not live without meaning, or at least without pursuing meaning, we must conclude that our inescapable compulsion to seek meaning is intended by the source of our being: God means us to be and to make our choices in relation to Him. God is immanent.

Transcendence and immanence cannot, apparently, both be true, yet neither can be false. This paradox does not therefore present an either/or (disjunctive) proposition. By reason we find that God is ineffably transcendent. Longing for meaning, we find that God is inexplicably immanent. And because we cannot honestly conceive of or embrace a life in which both reason and the longing for meaning are nothing, we conclude that God is, impossibly but necessarily, both transcendent *and* immanent. God is one (or, for Christians, three-in-one, which might be thought of as the transcendent, the immanent, and the relation between them). God is revealed in us, but we are not God. But how can that be? We are thus confronted by a mysterious paradox which the human mind is incapable of either escaping or resolving. We live with it, if we are not to lie down and die in the dark, striving to imagine the unimaginable, created to live, within paradox, in relation to the mysterious One that includes us.

3. Justice and Mercy

Two other qualities both ascribed to the divine that would seem to be mutually exclusive (see "Transcendence and Immanence," page 3) are justice and mercy. Both are also ascribed to any worldly ruler—king or judge—whom we call good.

The extreme of justice is the ancient ideal of repaying debt, giving each his due, tit for tat, an eye for an eye or its equivalent in monetary compensation. In human beings, particularly in aristocratic societies, unmoderated commitment to such justice very easily edges into revenge, of which one of the fruits is the historical feuding between the likes of the Capulets and the Montagues or the Hatfields and the McCoys. The contrary extreme of mercy may be seen in the love of Christ for all men, who are also his enemies, or in the infinite compassion of the Buddha. In human beings, unmoderated commitment to such mercy can very easily edge into a willful or sentimental blindness that allows offenders to "get away with" their offenses, thus encouraging repetition of offenses and neglecting mercy toward victims, of which the fruit is the collapse of order, and consequently of trust, in the community. How could the single ruler, of a city or of the world, possibly rule with both such justice and such mercy?

A guilty thief comes before a judge. Assuming the facts of the case are clear, the judge may either punish the thief, which is justice, or not punish him, which is mercy. Perfect justice demands that he be punished. Perfect mercy demands that he not be punished. And every just judgment will be considered merciless by the friends of the thief; every merciful one will be considered unjust by the friends of the thief's victim. (As I heard Mary Holmes say, "We want mercy for ourselves and justice for our enemies.") How can a judge be both just and merciful?

In human practice, of course, judges consider the circumstances, exacerbating or extenuating, and also the penitence or impenitence of the guilty party, penitence generally inviting mercy, impenitence inviting justice. The ideal becomes justice tempered with mercy in a judgment involving some form of practical adjustment between the two principles, depending on the particulars of the case: a sentence may be reduced without being eliminated. In the world of men, such compromises are required and make a kind of common sense. As Portia says in Shakespeare's *Merchant of Venice*, "in the course of justice, none of us / Should see salvation" (IV.i.199–200). Without the tempering of justice with mercy, we would all be in a parlous state. But unlimited mercy, man being fallible, releases evil from restraint and human society collapses into an equally parlous state in the form of licensed universal predation. Hence every worldly judge or ruler whom we call good must be engaged in the tempering of justice with mercy.

Nevertheless, there seems to be no sense in which any such tempering judgment will enact either justice or mercy. How could it? A reduced punishment is neither perfect justice nor perfect mercy. Yet a worldly judge could never rightly enact total justice *or* total mercy. Total justice is merciless; total mercy is unjust.

In contemplating God, the case (if it can be called a case) is altered. God is *both* absolutely and totally just *and* absolutely and totally merciful, a recognition by which the mind of man is stymied. These contrary attributes of God cannot both be true, yet neither cannot not be true. The mind of man is thus driven to surrender in the face of its incapacity to conceive of the divine. We are forced to confess that only in the divine can such opposites inhere—to us unimaginably—together. The truth of this paradox cannot be experienced; it can be held in the mind only by faith.

4. Finite and Infinite

We are aware that we are finite beings midway between the infinite and the infinitesimal (hence, in part, Tolkien's "Middle Earth"). But we can imagine neither of those poles of reality, if that's what they are, or at least poles of thought. Nor can we imagine that the universe is either finite or infinite. No matter how far we send our mind outward into the bigness of outer space or inward into the tininess of space within the atom, we cannot conceive of either. Both, if not beyond mathematical symbolism, are certainly beyond the human imagination.

Even modern mathematics, which could not exist without symbols for infinite nothing (0), infinitesimal something (ε or δ), and infinite everything (∞), has relevance only to the finitude that we are and the finitude in which we live. The rest might as well be fictional play (of which the string and multiverse theories are good examples). The best science now reports that the universe itself and the world in which we live are balanced upon an infinitesimal point conducive to life and consciousness. Assume a minute degree of variation this way or that in any of the fundamentals that we take to be the facts of physics and we could not exist. Examples include the gravitational, electromagnetic, strong nuclear, weak nuclear, and cosmological constants; the initial distribution of mass/energy; the ratio of masses for protons and electrons and for protons and neutrons; the velocity of light; and various galactic, solar, and planetary conditions including the nature and orbit of the moon, plate tectonics, and the tides.[1] This infinitesimal balance point is one of the strong arguments for the intelligent design of the universe, but that is not the point here. The point is that human beings are aware and, under various mythologies, have always since the beginning of human consciousness been aware that we exist as finites among infinities.

We can imagine neither dying nor living forever. We can neither bear the notion that we might be ultimately meaningless nor rationally conceive any way that we could be ultimately meaningful. We are stymied by the

---

1   https://intelligentdesign.org/articles/list-of-fine-tuning-parameters/

presence of the actually finite within the infinite, and of the potentially infinite within the finite. We are that finitude that craves the infinite, comprehending neither.

5. *Halacha* and *Kabbala*

Every religious tradition seems to have two aspects, which we might call the rational and the mystical (or exoteric and esoteric, or theological and theosophical, or legal and intuitive, or public and restricted).

The word *mystery* in English comes from two sources and means two different things. One meaning derives from the Latin *ministerium*, meaning service or occupation (from *minister*, meaning servant). It is in this sense of a trade or craft, or a group of people who practice it, that the word is used in phrases like "mystery plays" (plays written and performed by members of a particular trade, profession, or guild) and "women's mysteries" (occupations particular to women: things having to do with menstruation, the birth and nurture of children, traditional home-making, etc.). The other meaning derives from the Greek *mysterion* (from *mystes*, meaning initiate). From it we get our word *mystery* in the sense of a) a religious truth known only by revelation and only partly understood; b) a secret religious rite and the cult practicing it; c) something not known or capable of being known, an enigma; d) the secret rituals or occupational practices of some body of people of similar trade, in which sense it often overlaps with the derivation from *ministerium* (as in "women's mysteries"); e) a fictional story involving the solving of a crime; and f) a quality or characteristic that cannot be understood or explained. It is from the Greek *mysterion* and the English *mystery* in senses (a) and (b) that we get the words *mystical* and *mysticism*.

In Judaism, the rational (exoteric, theological, legal, public) tradition is called *halacha*—literally, the way to walk or to go. It is represented by the divine instructions to the people of Israel in the Torah (Pentateuch) and the successive commentaries on it forming the Talmud and its offshoots, including those of Maimonides, who organized all the instructions of the Torah into 613 specific commandments, positive and negative. The mystical (esoteric, theosophical, intuitive, restricted) tradition in Judaism is called *kabbala*—literally, that which is received, hence "something handed down by tradition." It begins in the first centuries B.C.E. and C.E. as commentaries on Genesis and on the visions of Ezekiel, develops through late ancient and medieval times, and is represented most influentially by the combination of texts called the *Zohar* (by Moses de León, thirteenth century) and the teachings emanating from Tzfat (in English, Safed) (by Shlomo Alkabetz, Moses Cordovero, Isaac Luria, Chaim Vital, and others, sixteenth century), claimed to be secret aspects of the Oral Torah, given by God on Mt. Sinai along with the Written Torah. As Gershom Scholem writes in the article on Kabbala in the *Encyclopedia Judaica*,

> Like other kinds of mysticism, Kabbalah too draws upon the mystic's awareness of both the transcendence of God and His immanence within the true religious life, every facet of which is a revelation of God, although God Himself is most clearly perceived through man's introspection. This dual and apparently contradictory experience of the self-concealing and self-revealing God determines the essential sphere of mysticism, while at the same time it obstructs other religious conceptions. The second element in Kabbalah is that of theosophy, which seeks to reveal the mysteries of the hidden life of God and the relationships between the divine life on the one hand and the life of man and creation on the other…
>
> Once rabbinic Judaism had crystallized in the *halakhah*, the majority of the creative forces aroused by new religious stimuli, which neither tended nor had the power to change the outward form of a firmly established halakhic Judaism, found expression in the kabbalistic movement. Generally speaking, these forces worked internally, attempting to make of the traditional Torah and of the life led according to its dictates a more profound inner experience. The general tendency is apparent from a very early date, its purpose being to broaden the dimensions of the Torah and to transform it from the law of the people of Israel into the inner secret law of the universe… The kabbalists were the main symbolists of rabbinic Judaism. For Kabbalah, Judaism in all its aspects was a system of mystical symbols reflecting the mystery of God and the universe, and the kabbalists' aim was to discover and invent keys to the understanding of this symbolism.

The ancient Greeks, in addition to their state religious rites, engaged in semi-annual ceremonies called "the mysteries" at Eleusis and performed initiation rites into them for priests and for worthy young men reaching maturity. The details of the Eleusinian mysteries are unknown to us because initiates were sworn to secrecy and none that we know of ever betrayed that oath. Herodotus mentions but does not reveal the secrets,[1] and Thucydides reports that though Alcibiades was accused of betraying them in "mock celebrations of the mysteries," the charges against him, categorically denied by him, were probably trumped up by his enemies.[2] Based on what we do know, it seems that initiation into the Eleusinian mysteries served as the foundation of morality and good character and of faith in the ultimate reward in an afterlife for virtue in this life. Plato in the *Symposium* (209e–210a) has Diotima allude to these mysteries when she speaks of initiation into the mysteries of love and its higher or final revelation. Aristophanes in *The Clouds* satirizes them.

In Christianity, there is a great long and complex mystical tradition that parallels and intermixes with the evolving ecclesiastical and ritual traditions of the church. Key figures in the mystical tradition include, among many others, St. Augustine, St. Francis, Meister Eckhart, Julian of Norwich, Thomas à Kempis, Teresa of Ávila, and John of the Cross.

Islam has a mystical tradition known as Sufism. Hinduism's mystical traditions are many and, somewhat as in Christianity, complexly interwoven with the rationalist traditions; one is Tantrism. In China, one might distinguish Confucianism as essentially rational (with mystical offshoots) and Taoism as essentially mystical (with rational elements). Buddhism also has a complex mixture of rational and mystical; its specifically mystical traditions include, in India, Tantrism, which it shares with Hinduism, and in the Far East, Zen.

One might develop the thesis that these two aspects of religion apply even to the quasi-religious worship that is modern science. There is the rational science taught in schools at all but the highest levels, and there are the mystical doctrines whose secrets are accessible only to initiates in the most abstract tools of higher mathematics used to address the "mysteries" of quantum and post-quantum physics, the origins of the universe, and the interface between physics and consciousness. Of course to non-initiates such a scientific mysticism sounds like fiction, as all mysticism must. And perhaps it *is* fiction, or fiction constructed in the service of earnestly held beliefs about reality (see "Pattern-Discerning and Pattern-Making," page 29).

---

1 Herodotus, *The Histories*, 2.171.
2 Thucydides, *The Peloponnesian War*, 6.27–29.

Finally, modern America now seems starkly divided between adherents to one or another form of religious tradition (Jewish, Christian, Muslim, Hindu, Buddhist, Taoist, etc.) and adherents to various forms of secularism (humanism, materialism, Marxism and neo-Marxism, utilitarianism, consumerism, commercialism, ecologism, etc.). There is no doubt a case to be made for there being both a rational and a mystical kind of secularism. Certainly there are both aspects in Marxism.[3] If we focus instead on what we might call "Americanism," that is the belief in the ultimate significance and value of the principles of the founding of the United States of America—natural human rights, individual liberty, the sovereignty of the people, limited government, equal justice under the rule of law, and the like—even among believers in these principles we might distinguish the rational from the mystical, between those who believe that such are the most rational practical principles by which a polity may be best arranged and those who believe also that the United States of America is a "New Jerusalem," a "city upon a hill," a nation (like Israel in the Bible) miraculously chosen and blessed by God, and "the last best hope of mankind."

This double relation to reality—rational and mystical—which seems to be characteristic of all faiths, appears to be a reflection of human nature, which in this way is essentially two-fold. Perhaps this two-fold nature is a function of the apparently bicameral mind: the left-brain establishing rules for the right way to act in any particular situation and identified with rationality, the right-brain providing a holistic relation to reality and identified with intuition. Or perhaps the bicameral mind and our two-fold nature are created to be receptive to the two-fold nature of reality itself. But if locating the source of our nature in either physiological sub-structure or spiritual superstructure—or paradoxically both—requires too great a stretch of our imagination, at least we can say that human beings, those creatures with souls who live in community (Aristotle's "political animals"), seem to crave both some kind of order to the externals of life—where to go, what to do, how to do it, what and how to eat, when and where to sleep, how to be healed, with whom to consort, what and from whom and how to learn—and some kind of path toward participation of the self in the essential meaning of ultimate reality. We are all beings both rational and mystical, both social and spiritual, both

---

3   See James Lindsay, "The Theology of Marxism" lectures (https://newdiscourses.com/2022/01/theology-marxism/).

practically focused and craving illumination. We crave to live well in the here and now; we crave to participate in eternity.

Within the realm of time, there seems to be no possible harmonious stasis in the relation of these two kinds of tradition in any group or in the relation of those two aspects of the self in most individuals. Historically, rational and mystical traditions in all the religions compete with one another, often conflict with one another, one of these tendencies at times rising to prominence at the expense of the other, followed by the tilting of the balance to the opposite pole, any rapprochement between them being at best temporary. Similarly, our individual lives are governed sometimes by practical planning and decision-making and sometimes by the intuitive leap. Few of us live in a steady state of harmony between these two aspects of our souls. And some individual people are almost nothing but planning and control, others almost nothing but floating intuition.

Perhaps the doubleness of our nature and of our religions is not strictly speaking paradoxical; perhaps *halacha* and *kabbala* represent two aspects of reality, which can be approached in either way, or, for the faithful, in both ways in different seasons or at the same time with complementary intentions. There seem to be *some* men and women who have achieved within themselves and with their fellow human beings a harmonious resolution of the apparent conflict between these two approaches to reality, between the two tendencies in our nature and our religious history, and some who have been able to share the fruits of that harmony in the form of example or teaching, and have inspired others to imitate those examples or follow those teachings in the hope of achieving a similar harmonious resolution for themselves. For the individual such a resolution "once and for all" may remain a possibility. For the history of religions, such a "once and for all" resolution within historical time seems at best unlikely if not impossible, except to believers in an eventual messianic redemption.

6. Free Will and Predetermination

"I knew that was going to happen." "It was meant to be." "It figures." "Wouldn't you know it?" "What goes around comes around." Poetic justice. Fate. Destiny. Predestination. All through our lives, not constantly but repeatedly, we see signs of an invisible order according to which things seem to happen not at random but nonetheless independent of the choices of human beings. As Aristotle says in the *Poetics*,

> Even matters of chance seem most marvelous if there is an appearance of design as it were in them; as for instance the statue of Mitys at Argos killed the author of Mitys' death by falling down on him when a looker-on at a public spectacle; for incidents like that we think to be not without a meaning.[1]

Or, as Feste says in *Twelfth Night* (V.i.399), "the whirligig of time brings in his revenges." Extreme Calvinists assert that we are absolutely predestined by God though we live under the illusion of having a free will, that we can but pretend to behave the way a saved soul would be likely to behave while our ultimate end is determined not by anything we choose to think or do. And though stopping short of that extreme position, all peoples have seen inevitable forces working upon human conduct: forces of nature, of physics, of genetics, of climate, of history, of spirits, of the stars, of the Tao, of karma, of God. We live in a universe that we don't control, and our experience of how that universe impinges upon us includes a large variety of determining forces outside ourselves.

However:

Every one of us experiences life every day and all day as the business of choice-making. I may choose to get out of bed now or in another moment. Shall I answer the phone or the doorbell first? I can make this or that for dinner—which shall it be? Shall I buy an electric vehicle, or a gas, or a hybrid? Shall I vote for the lying crook or the naïve idealist? Shall I

---

1 Chapter 9 (1452a), translated by Ingram Bywater.

make the funny but nasty comment I have in mind or keep it to myself? I would rather play the cello than the violin. No, I will not marry that person; yes, I will do anything to be able to marry this one. One's whole life seems to be the pathway that has resulted from all the myriad choices we have made. Extreme existentialists have gone so far as to assert our absolute freedom of will, there being nothing to constrain it: no God, no nature of man, no rules.

Well, which is it? Are we caught in an order of unalterably unfolding events in which we play the role of victims or patients or beneficiaries under the illusion that we are making choices and determining outcomes? Or are we actually making free will choices that affect the outcomes and events of our personal lives and of the world, both visibly and invisibly, all theoretical constraints on our speech and behavior being mere excuses for ourselves, imaginary refuges from the unbearable weight of freedom of the will that terrifies us?

In *Pirkei Avot* Rabbi Akiva asserts both principles: "All is foreseen, and free will is given."[2] Just before beginning the Eighteen Benedictions three times a day, observant Jews say, "Lord, open my lips, and my mouth shall [or 'so that my mouth may'] proclaim your praise," implying that even prayer to God depends upon both man's will and God's. Dante, following Thomas Aquinas and other doctors of the Church, also asserts both principles: Man's free will is God's greatest gift to man,[3] *and* God predestines all souls (and everything else).[4] And like the mystery of why God predestines this soul for one thing and that soul for another, how free will and predestination can both be true is hidden so deep within the mind of God that no created being, even the highest angel, can comprehend it.[5] ("We can't comprehend what comprehends us.")

If we go by our actual experience—and what else, besides faith, have we to go on?—neither the extreme Calvinist nor the extreme Existentialist describes the reality of the lives of human beings, who must be choosing things all the time and who at the same time are aware that their choices unfold within an invisible structure of reality only minimally subject to their choosing.

Mary Holmes once said, "It doesn't matter whether we actually have free will or not; we *think* we do." The hypothesis that we don't is purely

---

2　*Ethics of the Fathers* 3:19 (my translation).
3　*Paradiso* V:19–24.
4　*Paradiso* XX:130–32.
5　*Paradiso* XXI:91–102.

theoretical. Yet at times our mental experience also throws our conviction of free will into question. "The devil made me buy this dress," says Flip Wilson's character Geraldine Jones. And we laugh. It's a good excuse. But our laughter at her self-justification is tinged with a deeper sense that we are in touch with a mystery. Maybe the devil *did* make her buy that dress. How can we know that the excuse is *only* an excuse and not also a form of truth? Can it be both?

Shakespeare's finally enlightened Hamlet expresses the paradox thus: "There's a divinity that shapes our ends,/Rough-hew them how we will" (V.ii.10–11). The poet deftly unites the two incompatible realities into a single experience, not with an explanation but with a metaphor. Yes, we have a will and make our choices. But in the face of divinity, all our choices are but rough-hewing. The shaping is not in our hands. One might wish to turn the metaphor around—perhaps divinity rough-hews all the circumstances of our lives and our choices do the shaping— but that doesn't satisfy our experience of the subtlety of divinity in its work within our lives. We are at best rough-hewers while divinity shapes exceeding fine. In any case, Hamlet's enlightenment includes the recognition that man, the choice-making being, whose choices are crucial in time and eternity, is at the same time subject to the shaping of a will that is not his own. By virtue of our free will we bear responsibility. In the face of the shaping of divinity, we must also learn humility, the lesson of *Hamlet*. As Mary Holmes observed, "Life either humbles us or humiliates us." We may rail against the paradox or take comfort in it, as it pleases us, or pleases Another, but its resolution, if it is to be found at all, lies not in time but in eternity, not in our minds but in that of our Creator.

7. Time and Eternity

By the fundamental nature of human consciousness, we live in time and are aware of doing so. And we are also aware that our span of life in time is limited. After our time, time may go on but we will not, at least not as we are in time. For each of us, whatever time is will cease. And since our primary impulse as beings is to live and to protect our being in time, we find the prospect of an end to our time, if not to all of time, to be problematic if not dreadful.

However:

An equally unavoidable characteristic of our consciousness is our imagination of eternity. As Philip Thompson writes, "[Man] is the one creature who believes that one of two equally inconceivable destinies will certainly befall him (and one of them certainly will), eternal being or eternal nothingness."[1] By *eternity* we mean not endless time backward and forward, not everlastingness, but rather that reality which exists outside of and containing time, a reality in which our souls, unlike our bodies, perhaps have a share. To say that we imagine it is not accurate. We cannot. But we can imagine something like the participation of our essences, our souls, in an eternity unimaginable. We can imagine that death is not the end of us entirely, but, as Plato taught, the separation of soul, of which life is an essential quality, from body, of which the decay and death are inevitable.[2] In short, we can imagine that there is life after death without being able to imagine it in any particular way, Dante's *paradiso* and Shakespeare's singing flights of angels notwithstanding.

What does it mean to say that time-bound mortal creatures also spiritually exist in eternity? That eternity is outside of time but time not outside eternity? Perhaps we had better consider the following paradox.

---

1   Philip Thompson, "Definition of Man (Late-Autumn Variety)," in "Reflections (Literary and Philosophical)" in *Dusk and Dawn*, page 199.
2   *Phaedo*, 106e.

8. Body and Soul

We know that we have bodies. We know that we are not merely our bodies. That aspect of our selves that is not the body we will call the soul (without any particular theological implications, in keeping with the nomenclature in use for several millennia—Hebrew: *nefesh, neshama,* or *ruach*; Greek: *psyche* or *nous*; Latin: *anima* or *spiritus*; Sanskrit: *atman*; etc.). So we say that we experience the self as composed of body and soul. What we do not know is how body and soul are related.

We experience having a body. In our bodies we experience pleasure and pain; we experience the craving of food as the body's hunger, the craving for drink as the body's thirst, the craving for sexual satisfaction as the body's response to the stimulus of internal drive and external perception, the craving for regeneration as the body's need for sleep, and so on. And we can address these bodily cravings by ministering to the body.

However:

At the same time our experience is that we are not our bodies only. We can be sitting still in physical comfort and yet experience joy or horror within the mind, experiences to which the body will respond, but whose origin is not in the body. We can discover or remember ideas independent of our physical conditions, and we can experience preferences that have no reference to the body. One might say that a preference for vanilla ice cream over chocolate is of the body, but what of a preference for Bach over Scott Joplin, or Joplin over Bach, for one who enjoys both? There are joys that are not the same as physical pleasure, anguishes that are not the same as physical pain. As Plato says in the *Phaedo* and elaborates in the *Republic*, we also have the capacity to permit or restrict the satisfaction of the body's felt physical desires. When my body clearly asserts its hunger, I can choose to eat or to fast. The "I" doing the choosing, the "I" that longs for meaning and eternity, the "I" that is not the body, we call the soul.

What is the relation of body to soul? To this question, so central to what we are, we cannot seem to know the answer. That relation is in us, but it is not accessible to knowledge or experience on any foundation but that of a priori assumptions not susceptible to proof, that is, on faith.

Several theories of the relation of body to soul, founded on differing a priori assumptions, have been proposed:

A. One's body, others' bodies, and the entire universe are nothing but illusion. This is the assertion of Buddhism. And the solipsist will say that all is illusion except the self's own consciousness. In both, the a priori assumption is the same as the conclusion, a tautology: if all is illusion, then I—body and soul—am illusion; if nothing exists but my mind, then nothing exists but my mind.

B. The soul is merely the temporary appearance, within particular bodies, of a single universal soul. At the death of the particular body, that universal soul or intellect remains what it always was. This is the theory of Averroes. Here again, the a priori assumption and the conclusion are one. If there is only one universal intellect, then all particular instances of intellect must be functions of it.

C. The soul is not anything but the body doing its thing. Emotion, self-awareness, choice-making, logical reasoning, imagination, dreams—all the phenomena of mental activity—are products of the physical body in operation. In Plato's *Phaedo* this theory is presented as a question by Simmias: is the soul merely an "attunement" of the body, on the analogy of the harmony in the sounds made by a correctly tuned lyre? Loosen the strings or break the instrument and the harmony vanishes. Similarly, stop a living body from operating (i.e., kill it), and the soul vanishes, ceases to exist. The principle was promoted by Lucretius in *De Rerum Natura* (which, however, despite its materialist vision, paradoxically ends with the worship of the divine Venus). In modern times this theory has been brought to the greatest possible extreme of explanation by neuropsychologists and evolutionary biologists. Any part of the self that we experience as non-physical is in fact the physical body invisibly doing what it does. Remove the body and there is no soul. The a priori assumption is that nothing exists that is non-physical, non-material. Hence, like the previous theories, this one begs the question: The experience of anything non-material must have a material substrate; any evidence to the contrary must be illusion, since materiality is all there is. One difficulty with this theory is that what materiality itself actually is remains unexplained. Reduce the human to DNA and one is faced with the question of why DNA does what it does. (The "explanation" provided by evolution based on the survival of random mutations over time is itself a theory held on faith.) And quantum theory, in which analysis resolves matter into "patterns of energy" and "forces," drives the concept of "matter" back into the realm of mystery. After Einstein, Heisenberg, and Schrödinger's cat, it is no greater stretch to think of matter as a function of mind (though not of the human mind) than of mind as a function of matter.

D. Keats called our life in the world a "vale of Soul-making," on the analogy of the "vale of tears" of Psalm 84:6. As befits the words of a great poet, the phrase is better than the intellectual theory of "Spirit Creation" with which Keats undergirds it:

> Call the world if you Please "The vale of Soul-making"...Soul as distinguished from an Intelligence—there may be intelligences of sparks of the divinity in millions—but they are not Souls till they acquire identities, till each one is personally itself. I[n]telligences are atoms of perception—they know and they see and they are pure, in short they are God—how then are Souls to be made?...How, but by the medium of a world like this?...it is a system of Spirit-creation—This is effected by three grand materials acting the one upon the other for a series of years—These three Materials are the *Intelligence*—the *human heart* (as distinguished from intelligence of Mind) and the *World* or *Elemental space* suited for the proper action of *Mind and Heart* on each other for the purpose of forming the *Soul* or *Intelligence destined to possess the sense of Identity*....Do you not see how necessary a World of Pains and troubles is to school an Intelligence and make it a soul? A Place where the heart must feel and suffer in a thousand diverse ways!...Thus does God make individual beings, Souls, Identical Souls of the sparks of his own essence—this appears to me a faint sketch of a system of Salvation which does not affront our reason and humanity.[1]

One of Keats's a priori assumptions is that previous religious doctrines of the soul are illusory and that only the human imagination has authority to speak on such mysteries. It is hard to see his complicated theory as anything but a Romantic confusion of the reasonable and the fanciful (see "Pattern-Discerning and Pattern-Making," page 29). Leaving Keats's theory aside, his phrase "vale of *Soul*-making" itself, seen in the light of Theories E and F, may have validity. It implies that, as in those theories, the human person is challenged to complete or purify or perfect his soul before going to judgment after death. Might Keats more

---

1   John Keats, Letter to George and Georgiana Keats, February 14–May 3, 1819 (his italics).

accurately, though less poetically, have said that this world is a vale of soul-testing or soul-purification or soul-completion? He himself uses the metaphor of the world as the school of the soul.

E. The soul is an independently existing being which, during what we call life, is imprisoned in the body. In Plato's *Phaedo* Socrates refutes the fear of Simmias that the soul may be an attunement of the body, and he goes on to give many additional arguments for the accuracy of his alternative picture: The soul performs functions higher than those of the body. The soul can order the body to do things against the body's apparent desire. A body only lives when a soul is in it, and when the soul departs the body decays into its composite elements; hence the soul is associated with life and the body with death. This also refutes the fear of Cebes that the soul may outlive the body without being itself immortal. Soul and body are independent entities joined for a time, neither losing its essential nature to the other, the body preserved in the form of a human being only so long as the soul is within it. There are various a priori assumptions here, one being that our experience of "higher and lower" or "better and worse" accurately maps differences in reality itself. Another, and the one perhaps most important for the subsequent history of human thought, is that correct reasoning about such experience will yield truth.

F. The body and soul are separate entities that at conception, or shortly thereafter, or at birth, are united into one single body-soul complex for the duration of life, a complex that Hamlet calls a "quintessence of dust."[2] At death the soul retains its higher (mental) faculties. This is Dante's principle, articulated in the *Purgatorio* and *Paradiso*, based on the reasoning of Thomas Aquinas and others. Dante adds that also at death the lower, physical, faculties of the body-soul complex are suspended until such time as the body is resurrected, whereupon those faculties will be called upon to operate again in an incorruptible resurrected body. In any case, according to Plato and to Jewish, Christian, and Muslim theology, in death the soul is judged as good or evil based upon its free will choices in life and is rewarded or punished accordingly. The a priori assumption here is the validity of divine revelation as conveyed in scripture and through its divinely inspired interpreters.

Digression: The evidence that impairment of the physical brain may

---

2 Shakespeare, *Hamlet*, II.ii.308. "Quintessence" is the fifth (celestial) element in Aristotelian physics, the four terrestrial elements being earth, air, water, and fire, earth being the lowest of the four and fire the highest. Hence Hamlet's epithet for man bridges reality from highest to lowest, reinforcing the notion of man as a microcosm of the created universe.

alter the personality seems to support either Theory C or Theory F, unless we posit several kinds of soul united within the human self, as do Plato (under Theory E) and the rabbis (under Theory F). Plato describes three souls wrapped in one: vegetable, animal, and intellectual. The rabbis also describe three souls wrapped in one: *Nefesh*, the lowest (the life-force within, attached to the physical world), *Ruach*, the intermediate (breath or wind, linking the previous and the following), and *Neshama*, the highest (the spiritual essence closest to God). To these three the Kabbalists add two more: *Chaya* (that soul in which ego is nullified) and *Yechida* (that soul that subsists in oneness with God). Exactly how physical damage to the brain and its consequent personality alteration or disorder would be accounted for by the composite-soul theorists we leave to them to delineate. On the other hand, psychosomatic illnesses, the well-known placebo effect, and studies of the physical as well as mental effects of mindfulness would seem to support Theory F. And we know that physical actions affect the mind: The physical grinding of the ink by Japanese sumi painters prepares their minds for the concentration necessary to their art, yoga poses prepare body and mind together for meditation, physical exercise will generally improve one's mood, and even a deep breath can often immediately alter one's perspective. Though at times we experience ourselves as both bodies and minds distinct from one another, at other times, and under certain disciplines, we may also experience ourselves as a single mind-body complex, suggesting that Dante's elaborately explicated version of Theory F has perhaps more merit than modern readers, who have grown up in the world of the Cartesian split, generally perceive. (End of Digression.)

If the soul is only the accidental product of material processes and biological evolution (Theory C), then what is the evolutionary function of human self-consciousness? Animal species apparently have done fine without it for millions of years. Alternatively, the world may be willed into being for the precise purpose of making a context in which human souls may perform some spiritual work (Theories D, E, and F). Then the question is why. Is it for the entertainment of divinity (a pagan notion), or out of divine love (the Christian notion), or as a test (the Muslim notion), or for a purpose that transcends all human thought (the Jewish notion, Maimonides arguing that the question is not to be asked because it is self-evidently unanswerable by the human intellect)?

Barring personal revelation, or the willing participation in one or another communal tradition of divine revelation, in our time and place, potentially liberated from compelled thought, the individual is free to ponder the question and to land on and adopt any theory he or she finds reasonable, practically useful, or otherwise compelling, and will do so based on some combination of influences in immeasurable proportion: upbringing, inherited teachings, psychological makeup, imitation of honored guides, life experience, and free choice.

What the individual cannot do is to choose based on knowledge of the reality. Being a body containing or united to or producing a soul, he or she cannot discern the soul's relation to the body. He or she is that relation and therefore can have no ground external to it for defining it, except the external ground provided by an act of adopting or leaping into faith in one of the theories above. Any such adoption or leap can be no invention of the self but can happen only as a response to a vision which compels, and thus the origin of such an adoption or leap lies hidden within the paradox of free will and predestination discussed previously. In any case, any knowledge we presume to have about the relation of soul to body must perforce be founded on some faith. Which brings us to the next paradox.

9. Knowledge and Faith

Reason implies the logical deduction of truth from true premises. When we ask for proof of something, we are asking to have what we don't yet know translated into a logical deduction from what we do know, from a still mysterious language into a familiar one. Once such a translation has been made, we call the fruits of it knowledge.

However:

There are no true premises (or facts) our acceptance of which is not founded on faith. For example, all of mathematics is founded on axioms, like the principle that if A = B, and B = C, then A = C. One either accepts this or all mathematics collapses. But it cannot be proven on the basis of any premise more fundamental. It *is* the fundamental premise. It is either self-evident, not susceptible of proof, or there is no mathematics. It is the same with physics. We can learn a great deal about the physical properties of matter and energy, but not if we don't assume, on faith, that the laws of physics are constant and unchanging. If that premise is not accepted on faith as self-evident, since it is not susceptible of proof, then there is no conclusion that can be drawn in physics. Similarly, to argue any matter logically, we have to accept the law of non-contradiction: The same thing cannot be both A and not-A in the same respect at the same time. A whole number cannot be both even and odd. The same animal cannot be both a giraffe and not a giraffe, nor can it be both a giraffe and a turtle. All logical argumentation is founded on such fundamental and self-evident premises—axioms (unprovable), not postulates (susceptible of proof). Without the axioms logic and argument dissolve; on the basis of them, we can come to all kinds of rational and true conclusions.

But reason founded on faith and leading to knowledge is not the complete story of the human intellect. Leaving aside for the moment emotion, intuition, dream, imagination, and revelation, even reason itself leads back to faith (or, as Thomas Aquinas argued, faith completes reason). This is because reason must inevitably lead to the recognition of the limits of reason, the knowledge that human knowledge on certain subjects—rather on all subjects—is limited and cannot by any method break through those limits. We all know these limits if we have spent any time thinking: The human intellect cannot conceive of infinite space or infinite time, or of finite space or finite time either. We cannot know from what state of being if any we have come or to what state of being if any we are going, what it means to be dead. We cannot know the future with any certainty. We cannot entirely know what it is to be someone else, or even know entirely what it is to be ourselves. We cannot conceive of God except as ineffable.

The word *mystery* (see "*Halacha* and *Kabbala*," page 10) names whatever is beyond the limits of human reason. It should not be, though it often is, misused to signify what we don't know *yet*. That reductive sense places all mystery under the government of future, if not present, science. It is the arrogant and foolish refusal to acknowledge any limits at all to human intellect, and it is particularly characteristic of our time of secular materialist humanism, which takes as *its* axiom that anything not materially observable and measurable by the human mind does not exist. The more useful sense of the word *mystery* is that which cannot be contained within the human mind, like the "solutions" to the various paradoxes we are discussing. In this sense, we all live in mystery. And we may add to Mary Holmes' dictum about paradox that if you cannot live with mystery, you are going to have a frustrating life.

10. Community and Individual

For most of history throughout most of the world, human beings have thought of themselves not as individuals but as members of communities: families, tribes, neighborhoods, cities, nations, religious groups, kinship groups, classes, etc. Aristotle defined man as "the political animal," that is, that physical being with a living soul who lives in a polis—which we often translate as "city-state" but which we may more pertinently translate as "community"—political, social, religious, agricultural, etc. And the individuals we know who distinguished themselves as individuals standing apart from the crowd of their time, say Socrates, Plato, and Aristotle, actually thought of themselves as citizens, members of their respective polis, and much of their thinking involved man's relation to the polis. The entire corpus of the Hebrew Bible characterizes the individual as primarily a member of the people of Israel, which began as a family and was meant to multiply while remaining a single entity, chosen by God to carry a message to the other families and nations of the world. Some religions, like Christianity and Islam, have tried to make the whole world into a single kinship group. All of this arises from man's being a social being whose primary duty is to fulfill a function in a congruence of communities—from the nuclear family, out through extended family, village, tribe, guild, profession, social class, religion, nation, to the entire world of men. The word *community*, which I've used to translate *polis* in Aristotle's "political animal" definition, comes from *com* (together) + *munus* (duty, function). Presumably we function together or we are not doing our duty; perhaps we are not even man.

However:

Since the Renaissance and the Protestant Reformation, human beings in the West, and especially in America, have increasingly thought of themselves as individuals. Governments, according to the Declaration of Independence, are established to secure the rights of individuals to which they are entitled by human nature itself and by God. Increasingly in our time we leave our homes and families and kinship groups to be educated or to work and end up establishing families among other surroundings than those in which we have grown up. We strive to move up in class. We study the cultures and traditions of others—historical others and present-day others. We travel. We compare religions as well as geographies and customs and languages. And even if we remain in the external communities in which we have grown up, we reserve the right to make internally our own individual choices about belief and behavior, in greater or lesser degrees of independence from our various communities, choosing among customs and traditions those which please us, as we choose foods at a smorgasbord. As a result, especially among the so-called educated, we have become a society of separated, often lone, individuals who must choose where to live, with whom to associate, what to believe, what habits to practice, and so on, increasingly defining ourselves not as members of a community but as individuals. This is individual liberty.

We know the downsides of these opposite forms of being. Within community there is always the danger of the community's having insufficient place for individual differences; it is all too common for communities to persecute individuals who find themselves at the margins of normative opinions or behavior. As a result, some individuals rebel and will often go to extremes of revolution against the community, throwing the baby out with the bathwater. Likewise, liberty untrammeled by communal norms of opinion and behavior leads to alienation and angst. Free-floating individuals find that meaning, purpose, morality, and self-worth, not reinforced by the reflection in other people, can easily dissolve, resulting in despair and suicide, or in fundamentalist or even fanatical re-entry into some constricting community. Perhaps the greatest challenge of our age is to find the right relation between one's individual self and one's membership in communities. Does such a balanced middle path exist? Or are we so constituted that we must forever be moving in the direction of one or the other extreme?

11. Pattern-Discerning and Pattern-Making

That the world is full of discernible pattern, independent of our discernment, we can hardly doubt. Night and day alternate; the sun moves north, then south again in a year; galaxies, pine cones, and mollusks grow in spirals; the hooves of a galloping horse strike the ground in a complex pattern of repeated order; rain falls downward and fire burns upward; each flower blossoming on a single rosebush, even in its uniqueness, is patterned like the others; groups of chemical elements share qualities; our hearts beat in a rhythm whether we know or observe it or not: "the boarhound and the boar/Pursue their pattern as before…"[1]

However:

Human beings, subject to patterns, already discerned or yet to be discovered, cannot bear chaos, which seems to imply meaninglessness. So in addition to the patterns that we discern, when we can discern no pattern in some phenomenon, we will impose upon reality patterns that we invent. Our made-up patterns at their best are consistent with those discerned in the world, but not all are so. We generally work in the day and sleep in the night because darkness makes work more difficult and seems to be conducive to the darkness of closed eyes in sleep. But is there in nature a pattern that teaches us that red means stop and green means go and yellow means caution? Perhaps. Why is Hebrew written from right to left, Greek from left to right, and Japanese from top to bottom? Men have seen constellations among the stars and figures among the constellations and the plan of the universe in their meanings. Where is the border between the discerned pattern in the movement of the stars and the imposed patterns of the daily horoscopes, whether written by genuine believers or by phonies? When the Kabbalists propose a ten-Sephirot structure to—well, to what? To God? To His creation? To the relation between them?—are they discerning or inventing the pattern? They also assign a number to each Hebrew letter. Is *gematria* then the discovery that because the letters of one word add up to the same number

---

1 T. S. Eliot, "Burnt Norton," lines 59–60.

as the letters of another, the two are therefore related homiletically? Or is it the imposition of a homiletic pattern upon a morally, spiritually, and aesthetically neutral fact (if such a fact exists at all)? Speaking historically, is Moses' prophecy of Israel's punishment for turning away from God articulated before the punishment has been experienced or after, a predicting revelation or an ex post facto invention? Does Jesus fulfill the prophecies of Isaiah or are the reports about Jesus a humanly constructed pattern to imply Jesus' inheritance of Isaiah's divine authority? Are we discerning patterns or inventing them? Is that lake we see in a mirage on the road through the desert a function of objective eyesight or imposed by a pattern in the mind?

Is there a difference? Perhaps mental life is a succession of attempts to discern pattern or to impose it. If so, by what pattern are we to distinguish pattern discerned from pattern imposed? Is such a meta-pattern even available to us? Or are we, also in this, comprehended by a reality which we cannot therefore comprehend? For the question arises whether in "inventing" a pattern we are also at the same time discerning it, not with the senses but with the imagination? What does it mean to imagine something? Is imagination invention or discernment? Can it be either? And if so, by what faculty could we possibly discern the difference? Ancient and medieval thought distinguished between fancy (the higher creative and combinatory faculty) and imagination (the lower and merely imitative faculty). Coleridge reversed this distinction, making fancy merely an "aggregative and associative" power and imagination the higher and creative one. Since then, imagination has been thought of as the visionary capacity to discern and invent truly and fancy as a kind of play not necessarily related to truth. But by what pattern is it that we may distinguish between the fruits of imagination and the fruits of fancy?

Are these discussions the discernment of a pattern of paradox built into the creation, or are we imposing the pattern "paradox" arbitrarily upon our experience?

We live within the mystery of pattern, and the origin and meaning of our own pattern-making, like the origins of the other patterns we discern in the world and in ourselves, remain a mystery to our rational capacity, though perhaps not to our imagination. Are we ourselves patterns imagined into being by an unimaginable pattern-maker?

12. Plato and Aristotle

Related to the paradox of pattern-discerning and pattern-making are two contrasting poles of the Western philosophical tradition. They may be understood as opposing responses to the question "What is real?" Are our perceptions of the world discernments or projections? Are thoughts more real than the objects of our senses or are the objects of our senses more real than thoughts? Is our experience of things derived from our ideas, or our ideas derived from our experience of things? If both, what is the relation between these two processes, and what determines it? Is it unidirectional or reciprocal?

The poles may be illustrated by the following pairs:

Pattern-discerning	Pattern-making
Platonic	Aristotelian
Idealist	Empirical
Realist	Nominalist
Deductive	Inductive

For Plato, universals (the Ideas or Forms) are more real than particulars. Particulars illustrate universals but also distract from contemplation of them. Plato deduces. For Aristotle, particulars are more real than universals. Universals are derived from particulars. Aristotle induces. Plato is an idealist, Aristotle an empiricist.

The Middle Ages continued to address this paradox in the form of the debate between the Realists and the Nominalists. For the Realists, goodness, truth, beauty, etc. are real in themselves and are revealed through particular instances. For the Nominalists, "goodness," "truth," "beauty," etc. are names that we apply to characteristics observed in aggregated particulars. For example, for the Realist, justice is an existing reality ordained by God, revealing itself to be present in the world in every just action. Realists are Platonists. For the Nominalist, "justice" is merely a name we give to a concept that we derive from the aggregation of examples of a certain kind of action. Nominalists are Aristotelian (though

Aristotle himself was more Platonist than Nominalist, believing that universals are not merely names but are real in their immanence within particulars). The Realist will say that the particular golden retriever named "Sonny" is a dog because the universal form of the dog ("dogness") is in it, or that it participates in that universal form, which exists permanently and independently of "Sonny" and of any other particular dog, which necessarily comes and then goes. The Nominalist will say that "dog" is only a name we give to a concept that we derive from all the particular dogs we have known or known about. If there were no particular dogs in the world, and therefore nothing to which to apply the name "dog," then the name and therefore the concept "dog" would not exist.

Well, which is it? In practice, if we are not philosophers, we accept both as accurate methods of thinking about things. When a villain seems to thrive in the world, we find ourselves hoping that ultimately justice is real and that eventually it will prevail in the villain's paying the price that justice requires. Observing a person returning a lost wallet with all the money still in it, we may say, "there's justice for you." Do we practice politeness because we believe politeness is a reality in which we ought to participate or because we were brought up to be polite? Is Sonny really a dog or is he a unique being to which we apply the name "dog" for convenience, believing that there is no such thing as "dog" but only Sonny and Rover and Fido and Snoopy, who share certain characteristics? Or is it both? And if both, how is that even possible?

Possible or not, the West has taken both Plato and Aristotle to heart, in some periods preferring one to the other, but never entirely renouncing either. Clearly the human mind has room for both concepts. Perhaps it even *needs* both. If we did not believe that Sonny is not just himself but also dog, we never would have developed a vaccine for leptospirosis in dogs. If we believed Sonny was only dog and not also his unique self, we could replace him with Rover or Fido and feel no grief. (The monster Descartes, among others, went further: Not only is Sonny merely dog, but dog is merely machine. This reduction of particulars to abstractions led to the apocryphal tale of Descartes nailing a living dog to a board and cutting it to pieces, its agonized cries being in the mind of the reasoner only the imitation of suffering, not actual, since a machine has no soul. This behavior might lead some to conclude that Descartes himself, or whoever did perform such deeds if Descartes himself did not, had no soul and was only imitating being a human being. In any case such behavior demonstrates to what lengths of depravity an abstraction can lead a man who has absolute faith in his own reason but no heart.)

13. General and Particular

Related to Plato/Idealism and Aristotle/Empiricism are the opposite but mutually necessary ways in which we experience meaning in any kind of art. We require both a general idea and particular empathic experience in order to appreciate anything.

Every fortunate person has had an English teacher write on an essay in school, "What is your thesis?" (or "What is your point?"). Why? Because among the billions of particulars our senses take in, we must distinguish the significant from the infinitely more numerous insignificant ones, and without a "point" to what we are experiencing, we cannot discern the meaning of those particulars; we cannot even register them. We not only cannot appreciate but cannot even perceive a particular without already having an internal hierarchy of value in place in our minds by which we determine (mostly unconsciously) on which particular to focus our senses. Crossing the street, we will focus on a moving car rather than a still one because a moving car can kill us right now and we want to live, whereas a still car, which could also kill us later if it were moving, is less of a threat in the moment. (And so on.) So, reading an essay, we want to know what is its point in order to determine its degree of relevance in the hierarchy of value that we all carry within us.

However:

Every fortunate person has also had an English teacher write on an essay in school, "Be specific." Why? Because seeing is believing. Being incarnate beings, we cannot grasp the reality of any concept or fact or idea unless we can experience it either physically or empathically (i.e., in our mind's version of our body—see "Empathy and Psychic Distance," page 42). Be specific, says the teacher. Give examples. Embody your argument in particular details so that the reader "gets" what you mean.

The unity made possible by the union of these two dimensions of any work of art, whether image, story, or argument, is what we experience as the meaning of the thing. The student essay must both make a point and illustrate it. Neither alone is sufficient to move us. Every particular word, poetic device, sentence, character, action, and plot development in *Hamlet* is essential to our experience of the play. At the same time, if there were no themes or universal ideas or notions about the nature of men conveyed by those particulars, we would find the play insufferably boring and insignificant. Meaning depends on the union of general idea and particular detail.

This leads us to the next two paradoxes.

14. Form and Content

Note: The word *form* here refers not to Plato's *Form* or *Idea*, the essential universal reality, but to something more akin to *shape*, an organization of matter perceivable by one or more of the five senses.

Outside of those mystical experiences in which the self is totally absorbed into the Godhead, there is for human beings no content without form and no form without content. This is because we are incarnate beings, experiencing the world in and through our bodies. Even thoughts, fancies, and dreams take shape using the metaphors from our experience of the forms of the physical world. Language itself is perforce metaphorical. (The word *language* is derived from the word for "tongue.") And we know, both from loving individual human beings and from our experiences of the greatest works of art, that it is precisely the unity of form and content, their oneness as we perceive them, that makes for meaningful experience. We know this from loving because if we try to tell a friend what it is that we love about our beloved, it is impossible for us to separate the beloved's soul, personality, character, and attitudes from the body and its characteristics at rest and in motion. We may try, but the result is inevitably unsatisfactory (often something like "what does he see in *her*?") We cannot and will not believe in a general statement unless it is accompanied by example. We cannot bear the boredom of reading a book on psychology that provides no case histories. And the greatest poems, the greatest music, the greatest buildings so thoroughly unite their meanings and uses with their forms that to try to separate their forms from their content simply destroys the experience of them as great works of art. The meaning of the Parthenon and its shape are one, just as the ideas and emotions of a Mozart sonata and its musical structure are one, just as the structure and sound of a sonnet by Shakespeare are one with its meaning and effect. This is why we say "seeing is believing." Being incarnate, without seeing we cannot believe.

Similarly, without believing, we cannot see. We do not and cannot register perceptions of everything the physical senses may take in but must focus our attention on one thing at a time. This is explicit in the anatomical structure of our eye, which vaguely registers light and shapes on most of the retina and in only one small portion can focus sharply. We must direct the movement of our eye toward any particular we wish to perceive in detail. The rest is peripheral vision. As with the physical eye, so with our entire process of perception. What we focus on implies choice (unconscious most of the time), and choice implies a hierarchy of importance—that is, of value. We focus on what we believe to be most relevant—to our survival, to our needs and desires, to our benefit or happiness, to our search for meaning. So that the most rudimentary of experiences of forms is governed by mind through idea and choice. Not only "seeing is believing," but apparently "believing is seeing."

Hence it might appear to be highly artificial to distinguish between form and content. It certainly *is* artificial to do so when we try to teach someone about a great work of art by prying form and content apart. The Shakespeare sonnet is destroyed so long as we are looking at rhyme scheme and alliteration and antithesis and metaphor and so on, and also so long as we are putting into other words what we think the poem means. Such analysis is a necessary preliminary to increased appreciation of the poem, but only when we put the parts back together again, cease analyzing and experience the poem as a whole, that is, only when form and content are again one and indivisible in our experience, does the poem spring into meaning and live in us. This is the reason for the wonderful (perhaps apocryphal) story about Beethoven and the woman at the soiree. After he had played one of his piano sonatas, she approached him to say, "Herr Beethoven, that sonata is so beautiful and moving, but tell me, please, what does it *mean*?" Beethoven replied, "This is what it means, Madam—" and he sat down and played it again. If he could have conveyed its meaning in words, he would never have had to compose the sonata. That fate and free will are inextricable, that human choices are made with partial knowledge and vast ignorance, that pride goeth before destruction, that one should call no man happy until he has died happily—all these statements may be true. But their truth has never been experienced or appreciated nearly so well as in the form of Sophocles' *Oedipus Rex*. And in no performance or reading of that play as written can they possibly be avoided. For human beings, meaning lies in the embodiment of content in form. Content without form cannot move us; form without content bores us. Their unity speaks to us with power and authority.

However:

Despite the truth that meaning requires unity of form and content (body and soul, vehicle and tenor, shape and meaning), we cannot help thinking of them as separate aspects of experiencing what we experience. Yes, she's physically attractive, but it's her personality I love most. I see what this drawing is trying to be, but the lines are tentative and lack conviction. That is a beautiful structure, but don't try to live in it because it will blow over in the first strong wind. We experience ourselves as both unities of soul and body *and* at the same time distinguish between our inner lives and our physical sensations. Sticks and stones hurt in one way; words in a completely different way. The spirit is willing but the flesh is weak. Geraldine Jones did physically hand over a check and carried the package home, but "the devil made me buy this dress."

At the same time that we are beings who crave meaning in the unity of form and content, we are also analytical beings who can see perfectly well that the two concepts refer to distinct realities. Two pianists perform the same Beethoven sonata on the same instrument. They play the same notes carefully following the instructions of the score. Yet one performance is thrilling and the other ho-hum. One played it so well that the sublime meaning poured through our senses into our hearts and minds. The other played it so drably that we were surprised at how dull Beethoven, in the wrong hands, could seem to be. The potential content of the sonata was the same; the form of the playing made all the difference. The second pianist's inferior form might well be the result of lack of vision and appreciation of the potential meaning of the piece. Or it could be the result of inept technique on the instrument. In either case, it was the inferior form of the playing that prevented the content from being delivered. And we know so if we have heard the sonata played by both of our hypothetical performers.

The difference between form and content, between technique and idea, is clearly represented in the development of any particular style of art. The history of a style, as Professor Mary Holmes taught, characteristically goes through a process of development from archaic, to developed, to late developed, to baroque, to late archaizing. And then it is over and can never be recaptured, though the same process of development will be recapitulated in some other style. At the archaic stage, the content or idea is all, and the artist is doing his best to make the form or technique convey it. In the developed stage, the form has caught up so that it and the content are in perfect harmony, content perfectly expressed in form,

form perfectly expressing content. In the late developed stage, the form begins to elaborate itself and the content begins to weaken. In the baroque stage, the form is doing nothing but showing itself off and the content is merely its excuse for being. And finally, in late archaizing, the artist, aware that the idea has been lost in the elaboration of technique, seeks to recapture that original content by returning to the earlier forms. This last effort, noble in intent, is doomed to failure. The artist knows too much, is too self-conscious. The real content has been lost, sacrificed to form, even to archaizing form. At that stage, the style is over, never to return except in imitations.

This process can perhaps be discerned in any style of art, whether it be in ancient Greek sculptures or Medieval cathedrals or Renaissance paintings or modern animated cartoons. And in this process we can observe both the essential difference between form and content *and* the triumphant accomplishment of their perfect union in any style at the peak of its development.

Here is some visual evidence from ancient Greek sculpture, but it comes with a warning: As Mary Holmes taught, "the greater the work of art, the worse the reproduction." Two examples below are Roman copies, which are always cruder than the Greek originals. And the reproducing photographs themselves, which are offered to make the point about form and content in the development of a style, must never be taken to substitute for the experience of the works of art themselves. There can be no substitute.

▶ Archaic stage: Marble statue of a youth, c. 590–580 B.C.E. Rudimentary technique trying to convey meaning, the idealized male human form as an image of the divine [image credit: www. metmuseum.org/art/collection/ search/253370].

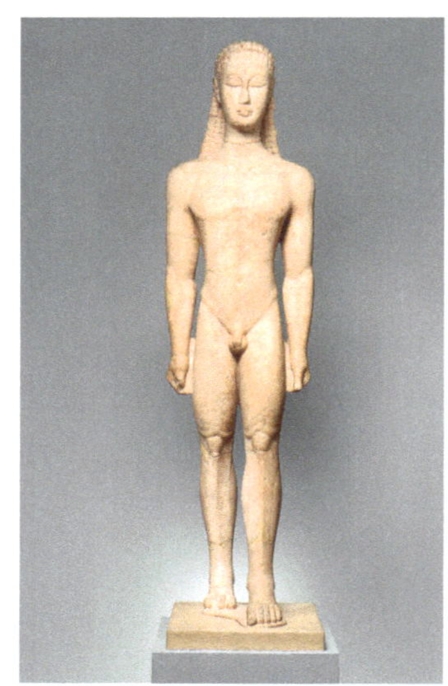

▶ Developed stage: Marble statue, the Kritios youth, c. 490 B.C.E. The technique perfectly expresses the meaning; the ideal, the divine perfection of a human figure, is made perfectly visible; form and content are one [image credit: https://upload.wikimedia.org/wikipedia/commons/9/94/009MA_Kritos.jpg].

◀ Late Developed stage: Discobolus (discus-thrower), second-century Roman copy in bronze of the Greek original in bronze, c. 460–450 B.C.E. The Greek artist (Myron) can now do technically anything that he wants, and still the ideal beauty of the athlete in motion—the union of stasis and motion, of divine and human, of perfection within the heroic contest (*agonia*)—is conveyed [image credit: https://en.wikipedia.org/wiki/Discobolus#/media].

▶ Late Developed stage: Doryphoros (spear-bearer), Roman marble copy of Greek original of 450–440 B.C.E. Imagining the Greek original behind this cruder copy, one can see the technique beginning to claim as much attention as the idea [image credit: http://employees.oneonta.edu/farberas/arth/images/109images/greek_archaic_classical/sculpture/doryphoros.jpg].

40

► Baroque/Hellenistic stage: marble Hermes of Praxiteles, c. 340–330 B.C.E. The content is now no longer the awesome presence of a god but the softened beauty of an ideally formed young man. The inherited sense of the divine is subordinated to the emotional effect achieved by the masterful technique: the heroic *agonia* has become *pathos* [Image credit: http://employees.oneonta.edu/ farberas/arth/images/109images/4thc_ hellenistic/praxiteles_hermes.jpg].

▼ Baroque/Hellenistic stage: Laocoön, marble of c. 200 B.C.E.–100 C.E. Here the divine harmony within *agonia* (contest) of the Developed stage has become the *pathos* within mere agony, and technique prevails over idea [Image credit: https://en.wikipedia.org/wiki/Laoco%C3%B6n#/media/ File:Laoco%C3%B6n_and_his_sons_group.jpg].

▲ Late Archaizing stage: Santa Maria Antiqua marble sarcophagus, c. 275 C.E. The technique of the style has now been forgotten or rejected in the attempt to recapture a divine idea. After this, Greek sculpture is over except as imitation. A new style must and will be found to convey a different meaning [Image credit: https://brewminate.com/wp-content/uploads/2018/01/011418-51-Santa-Maria-Antiqua-Sarcophagus-Art-History.jpg].

The history of a style illustrates our recognition that form and content are not identical entities, that forms evolve to convey meaning and then decay. Yet the fact that we experience as the most satisfying and meaningful works of art those in which form and content unite into a single experience—as in the Kritios youth or Chartres Cathedral or the Chinese painting called *Six Persimmons* or a Shakespeare sonnet or a late self-portrait by Rembrandt or Mozart's *Requiem* or Austen's *Pride and Prejudice*—may provide some empirical evidence in support of Theory F under "Body and Soul" (page 19). Perhaps it is for the sake of their union that we are given the awareness of the difference between form and content. Perhaps it is for the sake of the third thing made by their union that we are given a soul and a body.

15. Empathy and Psychic Distance

Related to the previous two paradoxes ("General and Particular," "Form and Content") is a fundamental paradox in our appreciation of works of art. It has been most cogently discussed by Professor Mary Holmes[1] and is re-presented in Chapter 15 of my *Appreciating Shakespeare*,[2] from which I adapt the following quotations from Professor Holmes:

"The basic foundation of all art is empathy, meaning 'feeling into.' Our empathic response is that capacity we all have to *feel into* what we are looking at, to intuit meaning in form. We are always exercising this capacity," whenever we are seeing or hearing or tasting or touching or smelling anything. When we see something, we are also "feeling what it feels like to feel the way it feels." If you see a person crack his shin on the corner of a bench, you feel it in your mind's version of your body. Your inner life experiences a mental version of that pain, and you experience something very like what the other person is feeling. You might even wince. That's empathy. It's not just the idea of his pain or the understanding of it, which you also have. It's the direct immediate experience of it inside yourself that precedes any idea about it or reaction to it. When you see a smile or a frown, a limping person or a scampering cat, "anything with a visible physical shape, moving or still, you empathize into it, knowing," in your own mental version of your body, "what that shape or movement or gesture means, because you know what it would mean if your own body were in that shape or were making that gesture. Empathy is the power to experience and recognize meaning in form, and we are empathizing all the time."

All art depends upon these empathic responses to images, sounds, and words. If we are not empathizing into the meaning of the forms in

---

1   See Mary Holmes, "Descriptive Notes to Art 5a" at https://maryholmes.org/wp-content/uploads/2022/09/Art-5a-Descriptive-Notes.pdf.

2   See Gideon Rappaport, *Appreciating Shakespeare* (San Diego: One Mind Good Press, 2022), Chapter 15. The chapter also discusses some additional paradoxes in the experience of art: "Escape and Return" (compare "Self and Loss of Self," page 50), "I and We" (compare "Community and Individual," page 27), "Integrity and Change" (page 55).

a work of art, we feel nothing. We don't "get it" and we're not moved. Being moved depends upon empathizing into what is moving us.

However:

We do not interrupt a play in which a good character, with whom we are empathizing, is being harmed by an evil one, with whom we are also empathizing. We do not step in to halt the cruel injustice of Othello in smothering his innocent wife Desdemona. And the reason is that we also have "psychic (or aesthetic) distance, the awareness, even while we're thoroughly empathizing into the scene, that it's only a play." While we are empathizing into anything in a work of art, we are also aware "that what we're seeing is art and not life. Thus, all art depends just as much on psychic distance as on empathy. If we did not have that distance, we would not be able to value any quality in a work of art. We wouldn't know it was art, something made by human beings… We would treat it as if it were life and would behave very differently in relation to it. Have you ever bumped into a department store dummy and started to apologize, only to discover that it wasn't a real person? You were empathizing into a work of art as if it were life. Your psychic distance was missing, and when it came flooding back, *you* felt like the dummy.

"In order to make sure that we don't react to a work of art as if it were life, every work of art must establish psychic distance in its audience. The work of art must do something to make sure that we know it is art and not life. And it does so by making boundaries. Painters put frames around their paintings; music has rhythm; statues are painted, made bigger or smaller than life, and placed on pedestals." In the theater we sit in normal clothes, in rows, in the dark, looking at people we know are actors, dressed in costumes, standing and moving in the light. "All these things tell us to expect to experience not life but a work of art. What happens when you ask a question of the guard in a wax museum and then discover that he too is made of wax?" The artist has intentionally removed your psychic distance for a joke. But there's no joke until your psychic distance returns and you realize your initial error.

"The coexistence of these two paradoxical forms of human perception, empathy and psychic distance, is essential to the appreciation of art. And you can see why by imagining what would happen if someone had all empathy and no psychic distance." It would be a form of madness. One would finish a Harry Potter novel certain that one could learn to do magic with a wand and incantations. "The opposite is also a form of madness." If one observed his neighbor strangling his wife on the front porch in the

44

manner of Othello and said, "This is exciting; I wonder how it will turn out," he "would be treating life as if it were art. It would mean that he had an excess of psychic distance and not nearly enough empathy.

"Empathy and psychic distance are not exercised separately in time." They are both working at the same time in harmony with one another, and the meaning of the experience, which depends on both capacities in us, comes through our exercising them, unconsciously, together. The unity underlying this paradox is the experience of meaning in a work of art.

*   *   *

These three paradoxes—particular and general, form and content, empathy and psychic distance—are ways of talking about the foundation of our experience. Break them apart and what happens to us is precisely nothing. That is, we can experience nothing, or at least nothing meaningful, in the absence of *both* halves of these paradoxes contained within any one experience of a work of art, or of reality itself. For even a car accident invites us to consider both the facts of what happened (particulars, form, empathy: running a red light this blue Chevy pickup ran into that green Toyota Corolla and smashed the passenger-side rear door, etc.) and what it means (generalities, content, psychic distance: the driver of the pickup is at fault; the Toyota driver has a valid insurance claim; etc.). Without the facts, there can be no story, and no insurance claim. And if you're not a friend, or an insurance adjuster, who cares about a driver and his error, innocence, or guilt, then the facts of the crash are insignificant to you.

It is in the relation between the particulars and the general, the form and the content, the empathy and the psychic distance, that meaning lies.

16. Beauty: Promise and Temptation

Beauty is irresistible and yet must be resisted. We respond to beauty in two ways; the first, if we are not careful, leads to the second. The first is a profound enhancement to life, the momentary experience and apparent promise of meaningful joy; the second is a temptation to enter upon a path leading to unintentional but inevitable disappointment if not self-destruction.

The first way is welcomed though unwilled. It is contemplation. We enjoy the experience of the beautiful. It fills us with wonder, awe, humility, love, appreciation for the fact of creation. It affirms the meaning of things, confirms that when God saw "every thing that he had made," he was right to call it "very good." In the presence of beauty contemplated we find it impossible to despair, impossible to deny the reality of joy.

However:

The moment our response turns from contemplation into desire of any kind, we are at the beginning of a pathway that, if we choose to follow it to the end, will lead to emptiness, misery, and despair. Because though the beautiful can be contemplated, it cannot be in any way preserved or reserved or repeated or used or owned. It cannot be possessed. The moment we seek to have, own, use, master, control, comprehend, or be redeemed by the beautiful in anything, or by beauty itself, we are doomed to disappointment. Unless we come to see ultimate beauty as Plato defines it, sacrificing all lesser beauties of body and worldly experience to the attainment of intellectual appreciation of the ultimate beauty, then every attempt of ours to make beauty our own is to be stuck on a lower rung of that ladder upon which, Plato says, the philosopher must climb upward from the beautiful thing to the beauty that is in it to the Form of beauty itself and ultimately to knowledge of the Form or Idea of the Good. And it is a rare philosopher indeed who can climb that ladder. But to be stuck on a lower rung, whether by attaching oneself to the beautiful object and attempting to rest in it, or by pursuing the beauty that was once in it to where it may have fled, is to be doomed to disappointment. This is the meaning of Keats's "La Belle Dame sans

Merci" and of Thomas Mann's *Death in Venice*.

Nor does it matter whether we find beauty in nature (a flower, a sunset, a landscape vista), or in persons (a potential Romeo or Juliet in the bloom of youth, a matinee idol, a Miss America, a fashion model, a porn star), or in works of art (a Greek Apollo, a Da Vinci Madonna, a sonnet of Shakespeare, a Parthenon, a Winchester Cathedral, a Golden Gate Bridge), or in a mathematical equation (Pythagoras's $A^2 + B^2 = C^2$, Einstein's $E = mc^2$). Beauty is in them, evoking our awe, our admiration, our love. But imagining that they exist for the sake of their beauty instantly vitiates them, turns them into instruments for a use for which they were never meant. This is why Mary Holmes says that a work of art may be beautiful, but beauty cannot be its purpose. Where beauty becomes the purpose of a work of art, the work will end up in toxic sentimentality (see "Caring and Not Caring," page 60).

We may think that the beauty which evokes erotic desire—it is not the only thing that does so—is a special case, for is not the sexual union to which it leads a way to possess beauty? Experience will confirm, however, that the beauty that evokes eros is but the subtlest, strongest, and least resistible of beauty's illusory temptations to possession, and for two reasons. The first is that though one's appreciation of the beloved's beauty may be renewed from time to time, the beauty itself is fleeting, for

> Time doth transfix the flourish set on youth,
> And delves the parallels in beauty's brow.[1]

The second is equally fundamental: Contemplation of the beauty that evokes erotic desire is perforce abandoned in the act of consummation, in which other kinds of attention take over, so that what begins as worship of beauty and grows into desire to possess it perforce mutates into something else (see "Sex and Love," page 49). That something else may be fleeting too or lasting, but in either case beauty itself has escaped. A man may be said to "possess" a woman in sexual congress; he can never be said to be possessing her beauty.

The experience of the beauty in the beautiful is a gift. So long as it is received with gratitude, it is real. The moment one tries to possess it by right of any effort, it vanishes like an illusion, and pursuing it becomes a prescription for despair.

---

1 Shakespeare, Sonnet 60, lines 9–10.

17. Male and Female

As Mary Holmes said, "all of creation is the union of opposites. All energy comes from the union of opposites." This is most obvious in the fact of reproduction through the sexual intercourse of male and female. Of course, because human beings are more complex and paradoxical beings than it seems that mere biology, as complex as it is, can account for, the sexual *relation* between man and woman, as opposed to the act of sexual intercourse, is also paradoxical at many levels.

There are many well-known tropes on the subject of the opposite sexes: the Bible's "male and female created he them" locates the two sexes at the foundation of human reality. In Plato's *Symposium* Aristophanes characterizes the two sexes as a joke: the gods split into two the original human creature, which had four legs, four arms, and two faces, and as a result each of the halves spends its life looking for its other half. Taking Sophocles' assertion in *Oedipus Rex* that all men, as the character Iocaste says, dream of lying with their mothers, Freud builds a theory of the "Oedipal Complex," according to which all male sexuality begins in lust for the mother, and its complement, the "Electra Complex," according to which all female sexuality begins in lust for the father. And Freud's question "What do women really want?" expresses the mystery that one sex must always embody for the other. John Gray's "Men are from Mars; women are from Venus" adopts the differing qualities of the two Greco-Roman gods and their eponymous planets to illustrate the paradoxical relation between men and women. Mars was the god of war, Venus the goddess of love and beauty, and they were (illicit) lovers. The Farrells liken men's minds to waffles and women's minds to spaghetti to illustrate the difference between the compartmentalizing of thoughts, feelings, and physicality that characterizes the mentality of men and the fluid interweaving of thoughts, feelings, and physicality that characterizes the mentality of women. And so on.

Mary Holmes observed that men think of women as being like children, and women think of men as being like children. She observed that the differences between men and women are so profound that it is almost impossible for them to live together in harmony, except that eros (combined with reinforcing culture) can have the power to overcome those differences and to hold men and women together nonetheless. Yet at the same time, the fact of eros makes men and women terribly vulnerable to one another, and that vulnerability results in the great fear of the opposite sex that characterizes both men and women—fear that is also overcome, paradoxically, only by the power of the very eros that makes them vulnerable. The differences, she thought, arose partially because men wear their sensitive genitalia on the outside while the sensitive genitalia of women lie within. Men are active, women receptive (see "Yang and Yin," page 68). Men, she said, have harder lives than women, and so are entitled to be served their dinner first, an assertion that gains some authority from the great speech of Katherine at the end of Shakespeare's *Taming of the Shrew*. Men live primarily in their minds and in their genitals; women live primarily in their whole bodies. Men want perfection; women want completeness.

And yet, despite these differences, "Adam said, This is now bone of my bones, and flesh of my flesh... Therefore shall a man leave his father and his mother, and shall cleave unto his wife: and they shall be one flesh."[1] Hence is marriage called a union, that single, overarching, mysterious reality that is the only fruitful human resolution of the paradox of male and female. And once again, that union is to be lived rather than comprehended. It comprehends us.

---

1 Genesis 2:23–24

18. Sex and Love

The fortunate (or gifted) among us have experienced the rare, indescribable, temporary, ecstatic union with another that is the union of sex and love. The *most* fortunate (or gifted) have known that union to infuse its vitality into the pre- and post-ecstatic fabric of daily life in relationship. Perhaps there are various degrees in the experience of that union. But everyone knows that for many people most of the time sex is not love and love is not sex. People engage in sexual intercourse without love; people experience love that is sexually unrequited.

Those, like Shakespeare's Iago and Sigmund Freud, who ground the higher in the lower, propose that love is merely the scion or sublimation of sex. The religious believe that as the body is a gift through which the soul grows into its purpose, so sex is the gift of a vehicle by which human souls may celebrate mutual love in the body. C. S. Lewis describes sex as a great wave that suddenly and surprisingly rolls into a previously calm relation of love, overwhelming and carrying the lovers with it. Cynics believe that love is only sex; lovers know that sex is an enactment of love.

Both in sex and in love, most rewardingly in their union, most people seek and many people find loss of self in achieving the self's desire of union with another self. And in so losing themselves, they may experience meaning in the reality of relation that cannot be experienced by a self alone.

19. Self and Loss of Self

Why is it that the self's greatest joy lies in losing itself? As in sex and love, so in meaningful work, in art, in play, and in worship, our greatest joys and profoundest experiences of meaning lie in those activities in which we utterly lose ourselves. We lose ourselves in work that we find meaningful and are good at. We lose ourselves in playing a game or a sport that we enjoy. We lose ourselves in experiencing a work of art, whether the length of our engagement is externally imposed, as in listening to a symphony or watching a play or a movie or reading a book, or internally determined, as in studying a painting or sculpture or architectural wonder. And if we do not lose ourselves entirely, if we do not forget the passage of time and the limitations of our bodies and our minds and our lifespans, then the activity has not satisfied us. If we do lose ourselves entirely, we return to ourselves, ideally, refreshed, perhaps illuminated, enriched by the experience. Of course we may return to ourselves despondent, angry, or otherwise vitiated, but we will soon seek another experience of loss of self that promises better.

In any case, we *must* lose ourselves or be driven mad with boredom, malaise, or horror at being limited within our unique bodies and our familiar, repetitive, unredeemed thoughts. This is no doubt because of the disjunction between our awareness of our limits and our capacity to imagine transcending them. For we live, and can only live, within severe limits, physical and mental. If the air around us gets too hot, we die. If it gets too cold, we die. If we go too far up into the sky, we die. If we try to live under water, we die. If we fall to the ground from the height of more than a few body lengths, we die. If we try to live without oxygen for a few moments, we die. If we eat the wrong plants, we die. If we let flying pieces of metal pierce our bodies too often or in the wrong places, we die. We will never again be shorter than two feet or ever be taller than ten feet. We cannot move both forward and backward at the same time. If we are males, we cannot experience being female; if females, being male. We must sleep or die. We cannot experience living in the past or in the future; we are always alive only now. And only here. We cannot be in more than one place at a time. Shorter people have played in the NBA, but if we are *too* short, we will never become an NBA player, however much we love basketball. We may study and play the piano for a century, but if we have no talent for it, our playing will never move an audience. We are our own unique selves and can never be someone else. As a wise man once said, you take yourself with you wherever you go. And, of course, our greatest limitation is that we die.

However:

While the animals live within pretty much the same limits, and also play and sleep, with the possible exception of dogs they do not worship, and they certainly do not make works of art. Why do we not only make and appreciate works of art but crave, perhaps even need to do so? Why is there no evidence of there ever having been human beings anywhere who did not have works of art?

The answer seems to be that human beings, in the midst of their limitations, imagine. We can imagine the absence and the transcendence of our limitations. We can imagine living in killing heat or cold; flying high or living under water in "an octopus's garden in the shade"; being invulnerable to arrows and bullets, like Superman, or being the size of Ant-Man or of the giant Jack slays. We can imagine changing sexes, as in Ursula Le Guin's *The Left Hand of Darkness*; living in the past or in the future or in other worlds. And we can imagine not dying much better than we can imagine dying. So that our mental life is potentially filled with images of our transcending our limitations, whatever they are.

Yet we know that we cannot transcend them in fact. And this combination of the fact of limitation and the imagination of limitlessness makes it impossible for us, unlike the animals, to remain within the limits of ourselves for long without thoroughly and repeatedly losing ourselves for relief. In fact, we *must* lose ourselves or lose our minds, and so we seek and find various ways of doing so. First of all, we all lose ourselves in sleep. We lose ourselves in work, in love of another person or a pet, in play and games and sports. We lose ourselves in daydreaming, in crowds, in physical sensations. Many seek to lose themselves in drink or drugs or danger. We lose ourselves in worship, when it is sincere, and in ceremonies of all kinds, if we choose to take them seriously. And we lose ourselves in any and all forms of art.

But we don't lose ourselves permanently, unless we do so in actual madness. We return to ourselves. And then, of course, the question is what, if anything, have we brought back with us? How have we been changed? Do we awaken from sleep rested and restored or more stressed and anxious or neither? Do we return to ourselves from work with a sense of accomplishment or of futility or neither? From losing ourselves in love do we return enriched and content or frustrated, disappointed, or anguished, or merely, once again, bored? Has our play been healing or harming? Did the binge or drug trip make us better able to face our limitations or worse? Returning to ourselves from worship, do we bring a sense of the significance or of the insignificance of our limited selves, lives, and world? And returning after losing ourselves in art, are we enriched or impoverished, more sanguine or more anxious, kinder or nastier, more hopeful or more desperate? (It is by these alterations in ourselves that we judge the value of any work of art.)

What then is this self that finds fulfillment in loss of itself? What is the consciousness of self for, that it finds frustration and even danger in too much self-contemplation (see "Consciousness and Self-Consciousness," page 1) and can find meaning and joy in losing itself in the contemplation of something or someone other—something or someone that is meaningful to the self but not the same as it? Is this an element in what is meant by "He who would gain his life must lose it?" Is our nature given us so that we will and must lose ourselves in relation to something not ourselves or else rot within?

20. Journey and Destination

We don't leave where we are, physically or mentally, unless we want to arrive elsewhere. Yet short of death, which takes us we know not where, the promise of every arrival fades and is followed by a further desire to journey further, or to journey back. Playing a game, we want nothing more than to win, and we are living in delighted loss of self in the attempt to achieve that goal. Yet not long after we have won the game, we are looking around for our next entertainment. The having won has nothing on the trying to win. We wouldn't play if winning weren't meaningful and important. And yet our joy lies not in the having arrived but in the journey. Being aware that one has achieved the goal is rewarding but for a moment, and inevitably less rewarding, less meaningful, than being in the process of striving to achieve it.

However:

Can we enjoy journeys without caring about destinations? And can we fully appreciate the meaning of the journey before we achieve its goal? Apparently not. We do find happiness in the journeying, but if we try to enjoy journeying for its own sake, we fall into sentimentality. And if we try to comprehend the meaning of our journeying in the absence of any goal (even if the goal is only to get lost or to be surprised), we end in absurdity. We can find motivation for the pursuit of a goal only in the perceived value of the goal itself. If we don't care about the goal, the pursuit of it becomes empty.

The relation between journey and destination is thus paradoxical. If there is no desired goal, there is no joy in the pursuit or appreciation of its meaning. Yet no pleasure in the achievement compares with the pleasure experienced in the pursuit. Hence the essence of this paradox is the relation between the journey and the goal.

The mystics instruct us to let go of our becoming and simply be. Our unfolding lives seem to demonstrate that we are meant to be becoming, for merely being, for all but mystics, becomes a bore. Death then seems to be the door into that state of being which simply ends our becoming (if we are nothing but accidental temporal beings) or fulfills it with ultimate meaning (if we are created to be eternal). In either case, our lives seem to be the repeated living out of the relation between journey and goal.

Is there then a greater reality that unites the two elements of this paradox? Is life itself a journey through time toward eternity, its ultimate meaning the relation between the journey and the goal? If so, it is a relation that remains unknowable before the journey's completion, whatever happens after. Unknowable to reason, that is, though perhaps available to imagination, and to faith.

21. Integrity and Change

Related to the previous two paradoxes ("Self and Loss of Self" and "Journey and Destination") is the paradox of the relation between the aspects of the self that persist and are consistent throughout a lifetime and the aspects of the self that change.

Some things that don't change: astrological birth date (which may or may not matter), genetic code, gender, fingerprints, predispositions to or talents for music or math or words or images or baseball, attraction to girls or to boys, greater interest in abstractions than in facts, or vice versa, and so on. The essence of whatever we mean when we say "I" is what doesn't change.

However:

Some things about us do change: most dramatically our bodies, but also our degrees of impatience or patience, our capacities to learn, to remember, to see patterns of reality, to appreciate art and literature, to understand other people and ourselves, to perform well on the piano or on the baseball diamond. All these may come under the heading of that about us which can learn and grow and also decline and decay.

Yes, we lose ourselves in a great work of art, and we return to ourselves when the experience is over. But we return in some ways the same self we've always been and in other ways different, changed, affected by the experience. Tradition has been better than science at tracing ways in which a self can be altered by experience and the ways in which it can't. But for none of us can either tradition or science substitute for our own experience of the growth or education or alteration or decline of the self.

This paradox is not really accounted for by the scholastic distinction between *substance* (the underlying essence—in human beings, the soul) and accident (the qualities exhibited by or the things that happen to a substance—in human beings, the inessential characteristics of a soul, the life experiences that impinge upon it). The reason is that the distinction between substance and accident is an abstract one, and human beings, mysterious to themselves, experience life as constantly messing with that neat intellectual distinction. Is the fact of my being moved or inspired by an experience of meaning a function of the substance of my soul, or of accidents to it, or of both in some relation? As a result, we are once again inside a paradox which we cannot comprehend because it comprehends us. So long as we live, we are who we are, and so long as we live we change, to varying degrees, with time, circumstance, and experience.

We discover on our own (or fail to discover) the mysterious unity that underlies the unique combination of integrity and change that characterizes every human self. As Mary Holmes would say (quoting someone who switched up the cliché), *"plus ce ne change pas, plus ce n'est pas la même chose."*

The final question about integrity and change is faced, so far as we know, only by human beings (who cannot avoid facing it without extreme difficulty and mangling of the self): whether the integrity of the soul is maintained in the ultimate change we call death.

Buddhists answer this question by saying that the self is an illusion. Finding that renunciation of desire leads to nirvana ("no wind" or "it blows out"), they aim to renounce even the desire to exist, answering Hamlet's question about which is better with "not to be," though even for the Buddhist suicide is not an option, for the desire to be dead too must be renounced.

In Judaism one may choose among several attitudes: In the Torah (Pentateuch) to die is to sleep among one's dead ancestors; in Psalm 30 "What gain is there in my death? Will the dust acknowledge you? Will it declare your truth [or faithfulness]?" In the daily prayers God "is faithful to make the dead live"; he will "take my soul from me and restore it to me in time to come." In Kabbala there are any number of versions of the soul (one or more of one's three or five kinds of soul) being reunited with God.

In Christianity it is in death that the soul "chiefly lives," as George Herbert puts it briefly and as Dante puts it at magnificent length.

In all but the mystic and the person of pristine faith, the one change the soul does not undergo on this side of death is learning what lies on the other side, in that "undiscovered country from whose bourn/No traveler returns."[1] We live with the question until it is answered by reality, at which point we either have our answer or the answer ceases to have us.

---

1 William Shakespeare, *Hamlet*, III.i.78–79.

22. Right and Responsibility

We live in the age, perhaps the end of the age, of rights. The Declaration of Independence of the United States of America asserts as self-evident that, by the very fact of being human, we are "endowed by our Creator with certain unalienable Rights." Those rights are then enshrined in the Bill of Rights, the first ten amendments to the U.S. Constitution. Since then, Americans have uttered countless times with perfect faith their "right" to this or that: "I know my rights"; "It's my right"; "I have a right to…"; "You have no right to…"; "equal rights"; and the famous "I will defend to the death your right to say it" (invented and put into the mouth of Voltaire by the British biographer Evelyn Beatrice Hall in 1906).

So thorough-going is our conviction that rights are fundamental to who we are that the claims to rights have been expanded into absurdity. The Universal Declaration of Human Rights adopted by the United Nations in 1948 goes beyond the rights in the American Constitution to include a right to healthcare and to an adequate standard of living. In his dissent to Olmstead v. United States (1928), Justice Brandeis argued for a right to privacy, and in Griswold v. Connecticut (1965) and other decisions the Supreme Court has asserted that right. People have claimed rights for labor unions, indigenous peoples, gay people, disabled people, medical patients, prisoners, men (as distinct from women), women (as distinct from men), children (as distinct from adults). Some go so far as to assert the rights of animals, even of the earth itself. And the political landscape of the modern world may be seen as divided between those who believe that rights can apply only to opportunities (conservatives, libertarians) and those who believe that rights ought to apply as well to outcomes (socialists, neo-Marxists, Communists). The ultimate justification for such a variety of rights goes unstated by those who have ceased to believe that there is a Creator who has endowed us with them. But the faith in the principle that we have rights remains unquestioned by all but die-hard Marxists (who believe that there are no rights but those of the utopian man of the perfected future society of their imagination, to

58

whom all other rights must be sacrificed).[1]

However:

It used to be that everyone knew that rights were attended by responsibilities. Just as you have a right not to be punched in the nose by my swinging arm (and I have a right not to be punched in the nose by yours), so we also have the responsibility not to punch one another in the nose. Every right claimed by oneself is attended by the responsibility to respect the same right belonging to one's neighbor. The founders of the American polity knew and asserted that self-government could only exist among a people whose fundamental morality was intact, that is, a people who acknowledged their own moral responsibility as human beings, a people who could discern right from wrong in basic human relations and recognize their obligation to act rightly, a people who were in fact more or less traditionally religious people. Without God and morality, they knew, as Shakespeare has Ulysses say in *Troilus and Cressida* (I.iii.116–24), that

> Force should be right, or rather, right and wrong
> (Between whose endless jar justice resides)
> Should lose their names, and so should justice too.
> Then every thing include itself in power,
> Power into will, will into appetite,
> And appetite, an universal wolf
> (So doubly seconded with will and power),
> Must make perforce an universal prey,
> And last eat up himself.

The abandonment of the felt moral responsibility that must accompany and sustain the enjoyment of rights must necessarily lead to the vitiation of those rights. And this is what we are seeing happen increasingly as rights are first weakened by being extended beyond reasonable applications of the concept and then overturned in the name of the struggle for power among conflicting interests.

In primitive societies people bore responsibilities with few rights. In an ideal American society, people would bear equally the burdens of responsibility and the benefits of rights. In an age in which responsibility is entirely cast off in favor of infinitely extended rights, the return to a tyrannical abolishment of all rights and the imposition of absolute

---

1 Lindsay, op.cit.

obedience to unchosen responsibilities becomes inevitable.

At the end of his notes on the Constitutional Convention, Dr. James McHenry, a delegate, recorded that Mrs. Elizabeth Willing Powel asked Benjamin Franklin, "Well, Doctor, what have we got, a republic or a monarchy?" Benjamin Franklin famously replied, "A republic, if you can keep it." If we choose not to live with the paradoxical combination of right and responsibility, we will end up having hard lives indeed.

23. Caring and Not Caring

"Teach us to care and not to care," Mary Holmes quoted from T. S. Eliot's "Ash Wednesday," asserting it to be one of the greatest of prayers. What can it mean?

We must care or die. We must care to eat, to sleep, to move, to satisfy or to sublimate the sex drive, to find some way to live happily ever after. If we have been gifted with civilization, we must also care about our parents, our siblings, our children, our friends, our teachers and our students, our patients or clients or customers. We must care about our neighbors as we care about ourselves. To some extent we must care even about the many whom we don't know. We must care about the past or, as Santayana suggested, we remain doomed to repeat our failures and overturn our successes. We must care about the future or fall into aimlessness. The children whose mother doesn't care to keep them fed, healthy, and loved, whose father doesn't care to train their behavior and teach them civilization, are destroyed as human beings unless they happen upon someone who does care. Not to care is to do harm to those who depend on us and to wither away in despair. Not to care at all is death.

However:

We can care too much. If we care about food so much that we must be always eating everything, or so much that we permit ourselves to eat almost nothing, or so much that we refuse to share our food, or so much that we spend our waking hours thinking about nothing but food, then we become monsters. The same is true of caring too much about rest and sleep, about sex, about possessions, about health, about comfort, about length of life, about the past, about the future. The mother who cares so much to possess her children that she cannot let them grow up to leave her, the father who cares so much about his children's future that he cannot see their unique gifts now—these too are monsters. We harm others and impoverish and eventually destroy ourselves by caring too much.

As Ecclesiastes might have put it, there is a time for caring and a time for letting go of care. The answer to the question how much to care about this or that, in this moment or that, lies in wisdom. Knowing that answer in each case is perhaps what we mean by the word *wisdom*.

24. Is Denmark a Prison?

> Hamlet: What have you…deserved at the hands of fortune, that she sends you to prison hither?… Denmark's a prison…
> Rosencrantz: Then is the world one.
> Hamlet: A goodly one, in which there are many confines, wards, and dungeons, Denmark being one o' th' worst.
> Rosencrantz: We think not so, my lord.
> Hamlet: Why then 'tis none to you; for there is nothing either good or bad but thinking makes it so. To me it is a prison.[1]

Hamlet does not (cannot) mean that everything is relative, that there are no absolute values and no fixed reality. He means that human experience is never merely subjective or merely objective but always relational:

Denmark is no prison for the cheerful; it is a dark prison for the melancholy. For mutual lovers eros is a joy; for the unrequited, a torment. Health recovered evokes relief, gratitude, even celebration; health lost may evoke misery, anger, even despair. To the mystic the world is a garden of delights, full of birth, growth, and flowering, and heaven a "brave o'erhanging firmament, [a] majestical roof fretted with golden fire." To the cynic the world is a cess pit of corruption, and the heavens "a foul and pestilent congregation of vapors." In one mood man is the microcosm of the universe, a masterpiece of creation, "noble in reason," "infinite in faculties," "in form and moving…express and admirable, in action… like an angel, in apprehension…like a god, the beauty of the world, the paragon of animals."[2] In another mood man is a worm, mankind's "heroes are as nothing," his "illustrious as non-existent," his "wise as devoid of wisdom," his "visionaries as empty," his "pre-eminence over the animals nought, for all is vain."[3] For Leontes and Hermione life is the story of ultimate joy and the exultation of "precious winners."[4] For Macbeth life

---

1 *Hamlet*, II.ii.239–51.
2 *Hamlet*, II.ii.299–308.
3 Hebrew prayer book and Ecclesiastes 3:19.
4 William Shakespeare, *The Winter's Tale* V.iii.13–31.

"is a tale / Told by an idiot, full of sound and fury, / Signifying nothing."[5]

The Lubavitcher Rebbe said, "Think good and it will be good." This is absurd if one takes it to mean that one's mere attitude can change the world from what one doesn't want it to be into what one does want it to be. I can't make someone love me by thinking he or she already does. I can't stop a war by thinking it will stop. But he is not in fact advocating wishful thinking or self-delusion. What he does mean, I presume, is that altering the way one thinks about anything alters one's experience of its meaning. If I think of my beloved as an unattained possession, my unrequited love is a prison. If, however, I can realize that love is a gift, that perhaps I need to become a worthier lover or that my beloved's happiness may be increased by someone who is not me and that virtue calls not for possession but for letting go—if I think good in that way—then perhaps things will be good, for both me and my unrequiting beloved. If I think of a war as a call to be brave and virtuous, perhaps I can help to bring something good out of its evil.

Of course such thinking is always attended by the additional paradox within the mystery of my own thinking. Is my thinking voluntary or not? (see "Free Will and Predetermination," page 15). Is my mood alterable by me as well as by external circumstances? The Rebbe would say absolutely yes; it just takes practice at right thinking. So would a good clinical psychologist. And yet we know there are some people whose thoughts cannot be redirected to the good, whose moods are impervious to alteration. Macbeth is an example. The borderline personality perhaps, the psychopath and sociopath certainly, seem to be examples of the impossibility of "thinking good" for some people.

So perhaps our thinking itself is a relation—between the "I" of the self that is doing the thinking and the underlying realities that influence the experience of that "I": genetics, physique, physical health, upbringing, psychological make-up, past experiences, talents, desires, overall world view, inspiration, grace. And since we are inside that "I," we cannot be masters of that relation, or rather we are partly masters and partly receptors of experience, partly subjects and partly objects of our own selves.

In short, just as each of us is a paradoxical unity of mind and body, a "quintessence of dust" (see "Body and Soul," page 19), so is each of us a paradoxical relation between ourself and ourself, a relation that we

---

5 William Shakespeare, *Macbeth* V.v.26–28.

cannot comprehend because it comprehends us.

25. Athens and Jerusalem

There are two particular ways in which we may discern the union of East and West, to which Mary Holmes ascribes the inventive energy of Europe (see "Yang and Yin," page 68). The first, described earlier (see "*Halacha* and *Kabbala*," page 10), is the joining of an Eastern mystical tradition represented by the Eleusinian Mysteries with the rationalism, practicality, and visionary idealism of the Greeks. That union gave birth to the unparalleled flowering of the human imagination represented by the culture—politics, philosophy, mathematics, drama, sculpture, and architecture—of the high classical period of ancient Greece, and in particular of Athens. The second is the later union of that classical Greek culture with the equally profound but absolutely different flowering of a visionary recognition of the unity of the just and merciful Creator of the universe in the ethical monotheism and prophetic culture of the Jews.

In the ultimate singular reality of the Idea of the Good underlying Plato's philosophy we might see an incipient monotheism. In many of the ethical commandments in the Torah we might discern an incipient logic. But it was the communication that developed between the Greek and the Jewish cultures, particularly after the conquests of Alexander the Great, which gave birth to the frictional but fruitful union of opposites that became Western Civilization. Out of that communication came both the Talmud and Christianity. Because of it the tribalism of early pagan Rome was converted to ethics, civilization, religion, and universal principles, inadvertently spread by the growth of the Empire, and producing eventually the civilization we have come to know, to value, and now to take for granted and allow to be slipping away.

The Greeks gave us the idea of life as an *agon*, a contest. The Jews gave us the idea that that contest is judged by the just and merciful God. Together, they yielded a civilization that values life as both precious and profoundly meaningful, that has given us our fundamental values, which include the classical virtues (justice, prudence, temperance, fortitude), the theological virtues (obedience to God and his teaching; faith, hope, and love), the virtues of the wisdom traditions (humility, kindness, patience), and the conviction of our having a free will whose choices matter to the divine and to eternity. It has given us the principles of the rule of law, the value of the individual human life, the concept of natural rights, and the necessity of judicial systems. It has given us the arts of classical music, oil painting, cathedral architecture, the sonnet, realistic drama, classical ballet, and film. It has given us modern science and its offsprings: increased health and longevity, exploration of the physical earth and heavens, reduction of the dangers to and labors for human survival. It has given us the awareness of and interest in the variety of human experience in all times, places, and cultures and an endless string of -ologies by which we can come to know ourselves and our place, both humble and exalted, in the universe—humble in being but small and temporary bits of a vast reality, exalted in having minds that can think, understand, and choose between better and worse, right and wrong, hate and love.

All this has come from the union of human wisdom and divine revelation represented in the amalgamation of Athens and Jerusalem.

How we use these fruits to address the further paradox, that such a civilization may be thrown away by its own beneficiaries in the name of ideas that the civilization itself has demonstrated to be false and destructive—that remains to be seen. Some say we are living at the end of the span of history influenced by the "Axial Age" (around the sixth century B.C.), so-called by philosopher Karl Jaspers, the age that gave birth to Greek philosophy, prophetic Judaism, Buddhism, Taoism, and Confucianism, and that the new "axial age" will be defined by the so-called advancements in technology to the point where human life and meaning will be fundamentally altered by artificial intelligence, nano-technology, and other medical and scientific developments. Some adopt the perspective in a short story of E. M. Forster and believe that sooner or later the "machine" will stop.[1] Some fear that because of its own moral collapse Western Civilization will be conquered and overrun by an atavistic tyrannical power like the Chinese Communist Party or a new Islamic caliphate. Some, as always, expect the coming of the Messiah or the Second Coming of Christ. Many, especially young people, who have not yet lived long enough to learn that most "expert" predictions turn out to be false, anticipate total human annihilation by nuclear holocaust or ecological disaster or the crashing of an asteroid into planet earth. And

---

1   E. M. Forster, "The Machine Stops."

some few maintain hope that the civilization will undergo a reawakening and will survive to thrive again.

Human beings can endeavor to predict but cannot possibly know the future. They can, however, strive to distinguish between the virtue and spiritual gift of hope and a false sense of security, between legitimate concern about the triumph of evil and irrational fear of imaginary cataclysms. We live in between (hence Tolkien's "Middle Earth"), trying to discern reality, pulled in contrary directions by the paradoxical nature of life, intuiting or believing or deducing that within the struggle between paradoxical opposites we have the capacity and perhaps the duty to discern and participate in ultimate unity, the only possible source of that which we crave above all—namely, meaning.

26. Yang and Yin

The ancient Chinese wisely made of paradox an image of the whole of reality. The *Tao* is the one way of all things. The word *tao* (pronounced and sometimes spelled "dao") means "way," or "path," or "road." It is therefore akin to the Hebrew *halacha*, the way to walk or to go in accordance with the *Torah* (which means "teaching"). The *Tao* is the way to go for the human being because it is the way that everything—all of nature, all that is physical, all that is spiritual—goes. But the *Tao*, the way of all things, is both single and double, as represented in the image called the *tai-chi* (or *taijitu*), now sometimes called the "yin-yang" symbol. That image is a circle made of two interlocking and equal forms of opposite colors, one white and one black (sometimes one red and one black), each of which contains a small circle of the opposite color. The two may be thought of as teardrops; they are sometimes depicted as fish, the small circles representing their eyes.

Geometrically speaking, the line between the halves is the serpentine outline of two equal imaginary circles inscribed next to one another within a larger circle, the diameter of each of the smaller circles being half that of the larger circle. Each of the smaller circles in turn contains a still smaller circle at its center.

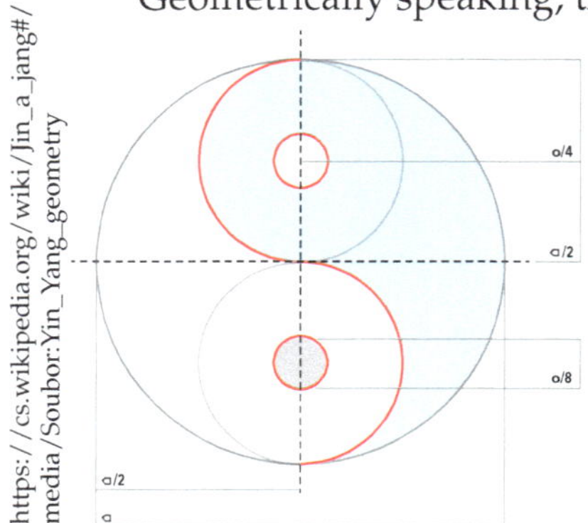

Some say that the curve of the line separating and joining the two halves of the circle is derived from the arc made by the lengthening and shortening of the shadow of a mountain or of the gnomon (vertical pin) of a sundial during the course of a solar year.

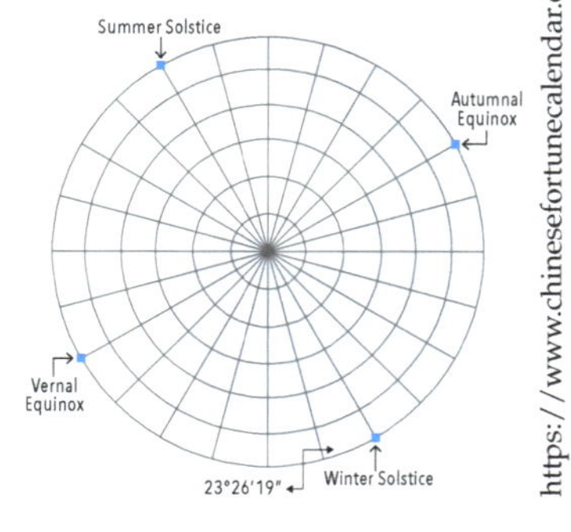

Some say that the geometric and mathematical relations among the parts of the symbol are built on the Golden Ratio (φ).

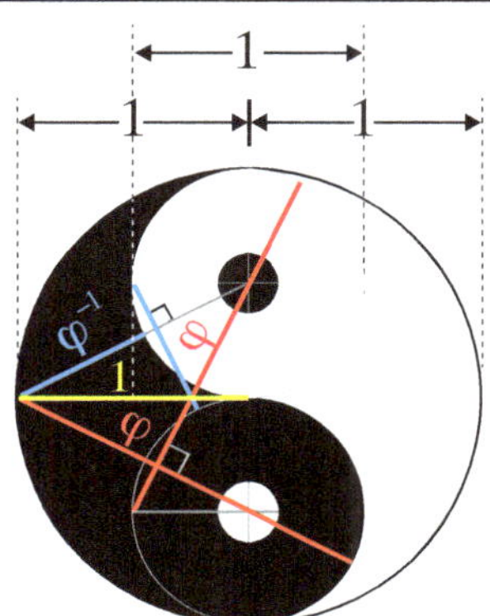

The Golden Ratio (sometimes called the Golden Section) is a proportion in which a whole is divided such that the ratio of the smaller to the larger part is the same as the relation of the larger part to the whole. In logic this proportion can be expressed as $b:a::a:(a+b)$; in algebra as $(a+b) \div a = a \div b$; in arithmetic as an irrational number designated Phi (φ) and expressed as $1+\sqrt{5}/2$, which works out to approximately 1.62 to 1; in geometry as a rectangle (called a golden rectangle) that, placed next to a square whose side is equal to the longer side of the rectangle, forms with it a larger golden rectangle. That is, the ratio of the smaller rectangle to the square is the same as the ratio of the square plus the smaller rectangle to the larger rectangle. This proportion has been known since Pythagoras and Euclid. It is related to the Fibonacci series of numbers in which each number is the sum of the two preceding numbers: one plus zero, one plus one, two plus one, three plus two, etc. (1, 1, 2, 3 , 5, 8, 13, 21, etc.). Building up a series of squares the length of whose sides correspond to numbers in the Fibonacci series produces a series of golden rectangles. A spiral drawn to be tangent to the edges of those squares, called the Fibonacci spiral, reproduces the spiral growth of many things in nature: the leaves on plants, the branches of trees, the flower of the artichoke and the chamomile, the scales of pine cones and the pineapple. Many see it as well in the shell of the chambered nautilus, in the spirals of galaxies, in every spiral growth in nature. Some see the proportion in the human face—the distance from the hairline to the bottom of the chin, divided at the eyes, forming the Golden Ratio. Platonists and Neoplatonists see in the Golden Ratio a congruence between the created natural universe and the most pleasing products of human art, and throughout Western history people have consistently found that the Golden Ratio produces the forms most pleasing to the eye (in architecture and painting) and to the ear (in music). The additional congruence of the Golden Ratio and the *tai-chi* symbol, as illustrated above, merits contemplation. [Image credit: https:// www.cut-the-knot.org/do_you_know/GoldenRatioInYinYang.shtml, Copyright ©1996-2018 Alexander Bogomolny © Svetlana Bogomolny]

Looked at from any point of view, the *tai-chi* image is profound.

The white figure represents yang, the black figure represents yin, and each has a small circle of the opposite color within it. *Yang* means the side of the mountain that is in sunlight. *Yin* means the side of the mountain that is in shade. Yang becomes the descriptor of everything that is active, hot, strong, moving, and masculine, and yin the descriptor of everything that is receptive, cool, yielding, still, and feminine. Here are some of the opposite forces, qualities, and characteristics represented by yang and yin. (The last is included based on an observation of Mary Holmes—see "Male and Female," page 47.)

Yang	Yin
Light side of the mountain	Dark side of the mountain
Day	Night
Sun	Moon
Heaven	Earth
Higher	Lower
Upward	Downward
Fire	Water
Hot	Cold
Right	Left
Direct	Circuitous
Straight	Curved
Hard	Soft
Solid	Pliable
Dense	Hollow
Container	Emptiness
Orderly	Random
Clear	Hidden
Even	Odd
Reason	Intuition
Form	Substance
Invention	Preservation
Masculine	Feminine
Active	Receptive
Action	Rest
Potential	Actual
Creating	Created
Cause	Effect
Purpose	Result
Function	Material
Energy	Matter
Change	Stasis
Perfection	Completeness

The *tai-chi* or "yin-yang" symbol implies that these opposites do not and cannot exist independently of one another but together form the whole of reality, that the relation between the opposite qualities is not a straight but a serpentine line, that each quality implies its complement, externally completing and internally containing one another. The great insight of Taoism is the assertion, implied in the very form of this visual symbol, that the whole of reality is a oneness made of the essential, necessary, and harmonious relation of opposites.[1]

We may see an ancient Chinese vase as a less abstract representation of this principle of the *Tao*. A container is yang; the empty space within it, which makes it useful, is yin. The shape of it is yang; the material molded to that shape is yin. The taking up of space by the vase is yang; the negative space created by its outline is yin. And in some such vases from ancient China, the very outline itself is the visible line at which yang and yin meet and harmonize.

An even less abstract representation of the *Tao* is the Chinese landscape painting, called in Chinese a "mountain-water picture" because it always depicts some forms of mountain and rock and some forms of water (falling, still; river, lake, ocean, mist, cloud). Rock is yang; it is strong and hard, supporting the high peaks, stable amidst clouds, directing the courses of moving water, containing still water. Water is yin; it is soft and yielding, as clouds driven by the air, as water receding down a mountain toward stillness. The stability of rock yields a pathway and ultimate containment to moving water (the dot of yin in the yang); the receding water actively carves its course through the rock over time (the dot of yang in the yin). Every "mountain-water picture" also contains a person or groups of people. They are all small, sometimes almost hidden, in relation to the encompassing landscape of mountain and water, suggesting that human beings, who exist as minuscule parts within the *Tao* whatever they do, can thrive only by following and thereby harmonizing themselves with the *Tao*. Resistance, which is possible solely

---

1 The emphasis of Lao Tzu's great *Tao Te Ching* ("The Book of the Way and Its Power") on the value of yin in the form of *wu wei* ("non-action"—or, as Richard Kirk puts it, "Don't just do something; stand there!") is in part a response to the imbalance in the world caused by the yang excesses resulting in the wars and civil conflicts of the "Spring and Autumn" period of the Eastern Chou (now spelled Zhou) Dynasty.

to human beings, can lead only to correction or to suffering. (In a common analogy: In a river like the Mississippi, you may decide to swim upstream or to swim downstream; either way you will be going downstream.) The "mountain-water picture" is thus always a representation not only of the structure of reality (the *Tao*) but of the appropriateness of humility in the human being's relation to it.

That the union of opposites is fundamental to the nature of things is a principle also known to the ancient Greeks, as may be seen in the masterpieces of the high classical period of the fifth century B.C.E. The Parthenon is perhaps the greatest incarnation of the union of opposites in architectural form. It is made to look most pleasingly rectilinear by having not a single straight line in it. It is constructed according to the Golden Ratio. It unites the shifting anomalies of human perception and the permanent stability of the material world in order to convey a visual

equivalent of divine perfection, balancing and harmonizing near and distant, curved and straight, high and low, tall and short, air and rock, light and dark, lightness and stability, delicacy and grandeur, beauty and ritual usefulness, and so on.

The great bronze sculpture probably of Zeus (possibly Poseidon) too unites within itself action and stasis, energy and rest, strength and poise, human and divine, potential and actual, and so on in the image of an ideal nude male human figure, the only kind of image that the Greeks found suitable for the depiction of a god. (Female goddesses were depicted clothed until the fourth century B.C.E.)

It used to be said that the only man-made objects visible from the moon are the Pyramids of Giza in Egypt and the Great Wall of China. Though not factually accurate, unless the telescopic lens is introduced, it is compelling as a mental image. The Egyptian pyramids, with their geometric and stone solidity, stand out of the desert landscape as proclamations of the human aspiration to permanence in defiance of nature. Are they not emphatically yang? And though walls are definitely yang in contrast to the spaces they divide, the Great Wall of China traces a long serpentine line, the result of an endless series of adjustments to the natural contours of the earth. Seen from high above, is it not emphatically a yin shape? If we take the pyramids as symbolic of the West and the Great Wall as symbolic of the East, it is tempting to think of the West as yang and the East as yin and the globe of the world as a three-dimensional

image of the *Tao*. Similarly, if we compare the Parthenon to, say, Angkor Wat—or the statue of Zeus to a statue of Buddha—will we not say that the *way* the West harmonizes opposites is yang in comparison with the yin way in which the East harmonizes opposites? Though of course both West and East are each both yang and yin, consider: The West pursues enlightenment through knowledge in the forms of mind-activating practices like philosophy, logic, mathematics, geometry, and science; the East pursues enlightenment through meditation in the forms of mind-stilling practices like repetitive chanting, yoga, and silence. The West's religions are monotheistic, active, and universalist, are based on direct instruction to men through divine revelation, and idealize the future; the East's religions are polytheistic or non-theistic, contemplative, and personal, are based on intuited instruction by nature and inherited tradition, and, in China and in some ways in India, idealize the past. The best men and spiritual heroes of the West are self-sacrificing instructors in divine truth, aiming to change men and thereby the world for the better: Moses, Socrates, Jesus. The best men and spiritual heroes of the East are self-improving exemplars of conformation to the structure of reality, aiming to harmonize with the world as it is: Buddha, Lao Tzu, Confucius. Compare Achilles (in the *Iliad*) to Arjuna (in the *Bhagavad Gita*), or Napoleon to Gandhi. The West seeks to assert the ego; the East seeks to nullify it. The West's negating temptation is to believe that matter is all there is; the East's negating temptation is to believe that *maya* (illusion) is all there is.

Mary Holmes saw Europe itself as a union of West and East, which she symbolized in her painting called *Europa and the Bull.* Zeus, in the form of a bull, carried Europa from

> the Asian shore of the Mediterranean…and deposited her on the island of Crete. She later gave birth to Minos, the founder of the Minoans, the first European civilization… The story symbolizes the radical bringing of the Eastern world into Europe, literally as Europa was carried there by Zeus… It is the wonderful union of those opposites that gave Europe the kind of strength that could pull it up out of nothing to be dominant. It was a cross-fertilization of the Eastern and Western worlds, and once it happened it could never go back... I think this union of opposites explains the marvelous fertility of Europe, the way it keeps producing extraordinary people and amazing ideas: knowledge of and interest in the historical past, romantic love, science, liberty— all emerged out of the same tiny part of the world over a few hundred years.[2]

There are innumerable ways in which the dot of yin appears in the West and the dot of yang in the East. The religions of the West produce yin contemplatives, and the religions of the East produce yang warriors. The West tries to moderate yang warfare with yin diplomacy; the East breaches yin diplomacy with yang warfare. We are all human beings. Yet it is nonetheless tempting to apply the image of the *tai-chi* to the globe of the world, the serpentine line dividing the yang West from the yin

---

2 *Mary Holmes: Paintings and Ideas*, page 77. See also "Athens and Jerusalem," page 65.

East running inexplicitly from somewhere between Moscow and Siberia, down through the Caucasus and the Middle East to the sea and then of course up again from the antipodes through the Pacific Ocean, perhaps along the International Date Line, toward the narrow space between the Siberian East (to the west) and the Alaskan West (to the east). The Greek images carried by Alexander to the borders of India left their profound stamp upon all subsequent images of Buddha, and the Silk Road brought silk, spices, and gunpowder to the West. The East's material poison, the Bubonic Plague, moved to the West. The West's intellectual poison, Communism, moved to the East. Both in turn have cursed the whole world. Are these exchanges the dots of contrary color in the *tai-chi* symbol that is the globe? Is the world maturing toward harmonious wholeness? Or is it heading toward a catastrophic lesson in the consequences of betraying that harmony? Is it doing both at once?

In any case, we are all going downstream in the Mississippi that is the *Tao*. The ocean into which it carries us, like the ultimate fate of Oedipus in Sophocles' *Oedipus at Colonus*, is known only to God. In the meantime, the wisdom of the *Tao*, as that of the religious and wisdom traditions of the West, remains: Paradox is of the essence of the human relation to the world and consciousness, and, at the same time, unity underlies all apparently irreconcilable opposites, unity accessible to the intellect as abstraction, to experience in art and mystical revelation, to both through faith.

27. Being and Non-Being

What are we? What is our life? What is our kindness? What is our righteousness? What is our salvation? What is our strength? What is our valor?… Are not all heroes as nothing before You, and men of fame as if they had not been, and the wise as without knowledge, and the sages as without intellect? For most of their deeds are empty and the days of their lives vanity before You. And the pre-eminence of man over beast is nothing, for all is vain.

Yet we are Your people, children of Your covenant…Therefore we are obliged to thank You, and to praise You, and to glorify You, and to bless and to sanctify and to give praise and thanks to Your name.[1]

or

Why are we here
If we just disappear?

We do not live yet, and then we live, and then we die. So it appears to us who live in time. What can non-being possibly be if out of it we come into being? What is being if, out of it, we return to non-being? What is the meaning of a life that appears to come out of non-being and then appears to return to it again? Is life made meaningful by the fact of the non-being that is its origin and end? Or, put the other way around, is non-being made meaningful by the fact of our lives that appear out of it and return to it again? There is perhaps no greater paradox than this that confronts the mind of man. And there is no human being whom this paradox does not confront at one or another level of awareness.

The word *Tao* implies that being and non-being form two parts of a greater—the greatest—whole. The word *God* implies that there is no such thing as non-being. From the human point of view, both are unimaginable, communicated only symbolically by an image (the *tai-chi*)

---

1 From the morning prayers in the Hebrew prayer book (my translation).

or a word (*God*) denoting an idea whose reality outside the limits of the human mind is inaccessible to us.

Depending on the assumption we make about the validity of the human point of view, we will come to one of two conclusions. If we assume that the human point of view is absolute and ultimate, we must conclude that all we know about reality is so much meaningless nothing. If we assume that the human point of view is limited and partial, that there is a point of view that is absolute and ultimate but is not ours, then we must conclude that being and non-being are mysteriously one in the *Tao* (the way of all things) or in God.

Or in both. For if we imagine stepping above the world and ask about the paradoxical co-existence in the mind of man of the East's *Tao* and the West's God, will we not conclude that the *Tao* and God are two fundamental conceptions of one reality?

*   *   *

The way of man is to meet paradox in awe and humility.

9 7 9 8 2 1 8 5 0 0 5 9 7